The Long Way Home

The Long Way Home

Timothy A. Herwig

tp

Published in this first edition in 2022 by:

Triarchy Press
Axminster, UK

www.triarchypress.net

A catalogue record for this book is available from the British
Library.

ISBNs
Print: 978-1-913743-60-4
ePub: 978-1-913743-61-1
PDF: 978-1-913743-62-8

Cover art by Chuck Meyers
https://chuckmeyers.com
Instagram: meyers.chuck

For Kathy and our son Forrest

Contents

You can see a map of each section of the walk at:
www.triarchypress.net/herwigmaps

Prologue

My dad has a talent for getting lost. We got lost once on a ride with my grandmother in the country outside of Albert Lea, Minnesota. Trying to find the way back home, we drove into the night. I sat in the back seat holding her hand. The darker it got outside, the tighter she held on, and the more frequently she corrected my father's driving. "Dick! Look out for that car! Dick, pay attention now; we're coming up on a curve!" It was probably the only curve for fifty miles in any direction.

And then it got foggy. "Dick, you better slow down; the fog's rising out of the fields." My dad kept on driving as it gathered in the ditch alongside the road. And when the road dropped down to the level of the fields, the fog was there before us, flowing across the pavement, pale and mysterious in the headlights. Driving through it, we tore it into tatters.

Letting go of my grandmother's hand, I got up on my knees to look over the back seat and watch the fog reform into a pale red stream flowing across the road, receding into gray as my father sped us down the highway.

At the time I didn't understand what it was, though I thought it strange and ominous, something like the green mist that killed the firstborn sons of Egypt in the film *The Ten Commandments*.

I have seen more beautiful landscapes than the thousands of square miles of corn and soybeans I grew up in, yet I have never forgotten that moment of mystery and wonder. Though I am middle-aged and battered by loss and sadness, I know that what seems monotonous and unremarkable, shorn of its native beauty still affords a richness of peace and quietude to startle the most injured and inconsolable soul among us.

~~~~

The landscape of the Midwest flattens vowel sounds. My mother's last name is Jobst, \'Jäbst\. Though the family still pronounces the J as a Y, as they do in Germany, the long vowel sound \'Jōbst\ did not survive. It requires the speaker to lower the tongue from the roof of the mouth, pushing out the breath through pursed lips. The sound vibrates from a point deep at the back of the throat. Pronouncing the vowel sound in \'Jäbst\also involves pulling the tongue down off the roof of the mouth. But the breath remains at the back of the throat, a vibration that sounds from inside the mouth. Only a little breath escapes with the final consonant sound, "t."

We keep things inside, those of us who live in the Midwest. Anyone who lives out in the open where little stands between you and the horizon knows this. It's all sky. It's infinitely blue in summer and hammering gray in winter. So you keep your head down and your thoughts inside.

Yet the landscape is haunted with memories. The memories of lives lived having kept everything inside. They seep out of us like a spring or the fog and attach themselves to objects, sounds, smells, the wind. They attach themselves to anything that can bear to take them.

Some of the memories we keep inside, some of them are terrible. Terrible things done to us, and terrible things we have done to others. We keep them down, and we run. We run so far and so deep that memory becomes forgetfulness. We're lost. We're lost to the living of life.

~~~~

I surrendered my seventeen-year-old body in payment for what I thought was life. He said he could show me the way back to life. I believed him. Like him, I would become real. My feelings were the road to freedom. He would help me, leading me to a specialness that only he had found, and I would, too.

But I had to sacrifice something for his counsel. Like all predators, he demanded my body, and he took it. All of his promises were lies, a pretext for devouring a teenager's emerging life. Years later, when it was over and with what life remained, I ran. I ran so fast, so far, and so deep inside myself that I forgot about time and living a life of my own making.

~~~~

When I moved from Minneapolis to Chicago in 1998, I was married to my first wife. She and I divorced two years later. I slowly recovered over the next four very difficult years. When I felt more myself, I wanted to affirm my new life. I decided that the right thing to do was to walk home: first to Albert Lea, Minnesota, where I grew up, and then to Minneapolis, where I spent my young adult life. I wanted to bridge my life in Chicago with the life I had left behind in Minnesota.

Late in the summer of 2004, I walked out of my apartment near Lake Michigan on the far north side of Chicago and kept walking until I reached Minneapolis five weeks and five hundred miles later.

As I walked, I was more concerned about getting hit by a car than with what was happening deep inside my soul. But in the months and now years since I walked to Minnesota, it has become clear that a great deal did happen. What you are about to read is an account of the inner journey I undertook, a journey that I did not know would happen when I began walking.

As the miles passed by, I became increasingly silent. I realize now that in this silence I discovered vestiges of a past that lay hidden and festering in my soul. A past that was far more disabling than the divorce had been. The irresistible compulsion I felt each morning to get going was this inner life breaking free, unwilling to stay in the dark anymore.

I discovered that I had walked out onto a landscape haunted by forgotten memories in search of my own. I found them again standing on a dock, extended out over a lake in southern Minnesota, facing a northwest wind bearing with it the cold air of change.

~~~~

The story begins the night of my third day on the road. I had walked west through the city, then the western suburbs, staying overnight with friends. At the end of the third day, I got as far as Keslinger Road just west of Randall Road. I spent the night camped out beneath a small clump of trees near the road.

You can see a map of each section of the walk at:
www.triarchypress.net/herwigmaps

Week One

Chicago, IL to Oregon, IL

A Dream

A pair of headlights shine on the tent. They pass, then red brake lights. The car turns around and makes a second pass. I get up on my knees to take a look. Is it a sheriff? As the car comes around, the driver sweeps a spotlight across the tent. Tires turn slowly along the gravel shoulder. The spotlight passes across the tent several times and then goes off. Whoever it is drives away.

What do I do?

I fall back asleep and dream.

My former wife, Michelle, and I scramble down into a narrow gully. A spring wells up into a stream that flows from pool to pool as it gently falls toward an expansive wetland marsh.

The marsh extends nearly to the horizon under a blue sky punctuated with towering white clouds. It is filled with reeds swaying in the breeze, birds and fish, and people either poling themselves along in narrow boats or living in houses made of reeds that float on the waters or sit on platforms resting on stilts.

Beyond the wetland, just on the edge of sight, is a wide lake on whose furthest shore stand summer cabins: a row of little white boxes resting on a treeless grassy lawn. Before each, extended out over the lake are wooden docks with boats resting above the waves on silver-painted lifts.

Little tropical fish leap into the air from the pools through which the stream flows, flashing bright colors against the blue sky. But the gully is now barren and lifeless, covered in black gravel and broken rock. Michelle fades away.

A thin man with long black hair and a beard walks down into the gully, pouring poison into each pool. The fish leap desperately to escape, only to fall back into the water and rise up to the surface, dead. Will the people living in the marsh and along the lakeshore be next?

I wake up.

Where is Michelle? How strange it is living a life apart from hers. I envy her new life in Minneapolis while I remain behind in Chicago, a hard place, living a hard life. There is nothing now between us, only silence and the past; no present other than the pain of dwelling too long on a life we no longer share.

I know the dark-haired man. The bogeyman out of whose mouth flow lies so potent that they still disturb my dreams. From sleep to blinding light, bent over and hiding, I awake his prisoner—living out a sentence that defies time and destroys love.

The Long Road Ahead

The sun rises into a hazy sky. The morning light is silvery gray. The pale blue sky is nearly invisible behind mists and clouds. The horizon is obscured by fog. There is not a breath of air.

It is Tuesday, August 17, 2004. Four days out. Walking west. I have traveled 60 miles.

Late that afternoon, I stop at Merritt Prairie Preserve. It is an L-shaped affirmation of native grasses in a monotony of corn and soybeans. A white service building stands at the entrance. No water spigot. A path leads from the parking lot down through a grove of jack pine, then out under the hazy sky. I camp beneath the trees. My feet are blistered, so I loosen my shoelaces and hobble off to explore in the fading light.

I follow a path mowed out of the tall grass that ends at a limestone block. It rests on a small rise facing north across open country. Interstate 88 is in the distance. How had the block gotten there? A truck or tractor, steel cable, and roaring engine. Stout men in overalls with large hands, wipe sweat from their brows and pull brimmed caps down over white foreheads, shading tanned faces, darkened by wind and sunlight.

~~~~

Across from the preserve and through the early morning fog is a seventies-era ranch house painted gunmetal gray. A broken-down decorative windmill stands in the front yard. A man walks from the house to a pickup truck parked in the driveway.

Walking toward him and holding out my empties, I ask, "Say, can I fill up my water bottles?" He tells me to go round the house to a faucet at the back. He gets into the truck and drives off. As I walk past the front of the house, a woman watches me from behind the screen door. I say hello, but she does not respond.

The faucet, with a long hose attached, is just below the kitchen window. After I turn the handle a couple cranks and wait, the water runs cold. The yard is cluttered with junk, and the surrounding fields are enveloped in a silvery haze.

I fill the water bottles and stand up. Just inside the window, the woman and a teenage boy and girl stare at me from behind the kitchen sink. I nod, then turn and quickly walk around the house and out onto the road.

Though the mists hovering over the fields gradually lift, the sky remains overcast and gray. The temperature is mild, but the air is damp and heavy. There is no wind. I am quickly wet with sweat, chilled and miserable.

All at once, the bromegrass that usually grows in roadside ditches gives way to tall prairie grasses and flowers growing in tangled profusion along the south side of the road. Farmers take pride in geometrically weedless fields. They do not ordinarily tolerate this tangle of wind-borne seed producers.

After a quarter mile, I see a concrete picnic table and benches on the left-hand side of the road. Pressed into the top reads an uncentered memorial: "Joseph Walter 1912-1992."

I sit down, drink a little water, and think about it. He must have been a farmer who got involved in prairie restoration. Maybe he was instrumental in establishing the Merritt Prairie Preserve. I imagine grieving friends and family members gathering on the anniversary of his death to picnic, recall his passing, celebrate his life.

~~~~

Malta is a small railroad town just west of DeKalb. I am hungry and find Brenda's Café. It is a small restaurant painted bright red. I take off my pack and stand outside for a moment to get my bearings. I have not bathed in a few days. I do not smell that good, and do not look that good, either. Though not ready to be in a room with a bunch of strangers, I step through the doors. The restaurant is filled with retired men and women, people taking their lunch break, a couple mothers and their children, and high school kids who work there and their friends. Most of them stop what they are doing, turn to me, and then begin talking about the guy who just walked in, me.

It is not long before they no longer take notice and leave me alone. Reading my maps, drinking one glass of water after another, I eat while looking for a place to sleep for the night.

~~~~

I stop in the middle of an intersection north of Malta. The wind rises out of the northwest and tears apart the gray mantle of the sky. Everything is sunshine, blue sky, and torn strips of cloud racing above green fields—light reflecting across the surface of every moving thing. The world inside me rises and falls like ocean swells of color and light.

Leaving the blacktop behind, the road changes to gravel and deviates from the grid, taking an easy turn to the west before dipping slightly down alongside a creek. A grassy green bank rises up along the left, and on the other side of the creek stretches a field of soybeans with a grove of hardwoods beyond. Under the influence of the open sky and windswept landscape, this sudden change unexpectedly transports me into the past—life on the open prairie, miles away from the nearest town, connected by roads that hold to the contours of the land.

It is now late in the day. I have been out in the open walking for almost nine hours. The clouds have returned, and scattered drops of rain begin to fall. A park lies beneath the grove of trees to the right. Ignoring the "No Trespassing" sign, I squeeze between the gate and a young tree, stepping over some poison ivy and beneath the shelter of the trees and out of the wind.

After setting up camp, I lie down, barefoot on the cool grass. Though the rain holds off, the wind continues to blow. Occasionally the clouds open up and the sun streams through the leaves above, casting a dappled, swiftly changing light across the grassy lawn.

Later that night a storm comes tearing through the woods. The tent is buffeted by the wind as thunder booms and lightning rips the night sky. Limbs come crashing down all around me. The voice of the storm comes roaring out of the whirlwind.

Frightened, but too tired to stay awake for long, I fall back to sleep before the storm blows itself out and moves into the east.

"A Steel Slab in a Prison Cell"

I have walked eighty miles west and have another fifty before turning north toward Wisconsin. This will take me through Lindenwood, Holcomb, Byron, Forreston, and Shannon, then north. At an intersection east of Holcomb stands an old house, a fertilizer plant, and a junkyard. Each at an angle to the highway as if constructed along a grid that no longer exists. A white Chevy pickup idles on the other side of the intersection. The driver is looking right at me. I wait. So does he. I wait a little longer.

A couple cars drive by, and then, sure enough, he drives across and pokes his head out of the window. "I just couldn't drive by without asking what in the world you're doing."

I tell him, "I'm walking home to Minnesota." He can't believe it, so he pulls over to the side of the road and gets out.

He is a big, red-faced, heavyset guy wearing a gray T-shirt and a pair of denim overalls. Though he cannot be much older than his mid-fifties, his hair is snow white, as is his handlebar mustache. He wears square-framed glasses and has an enormous mole at the tip of his nose. We talk a little bit about my walk, but when I tell him I had come up Holcomb Road, he launches into a history lesson on the area and his family.

He says, "Did you know that you are now standing on the former right-of-way of the Chicago Great Western Railroad between Chicago and Minneapolis?"

I reply that I did not.

"Well, you are. It cut right across where we're standing, running northwest from Lindenwood, where you came from this morning, on along to Holcomb, and then Stillman Valley on its way to Byron, where it crossed the Rock River. My great-grandfather owned land east of here that the railroad took possession of through eminent domain. Forced him off the land he'd homesteaded. They finally pulled up the line after the Byron Nuclear Plant was completed in the 1980s."

I ask, "Are there any good motels in Byron? I hope to spend the night there."

He says there are none, then reconsiders. "There's one north of town about ten miles. But that won't do you any good. Ten miles in a car is one thing, but I don't doubt that on foot it is quite another."

Not noticing the despair written all over my face at the prospect of sleeping outside again—no bed, no shower, no running water, dirty, dusty, and footsore (I had planned on staying two nights in Byron in order to rest and regroup)— he goes on, "There used to be a hotel in Byron, right downtown. Built years ago. Though not as grand as anything you'd see in Chicago, it was grand by Byron's standards. Well, they tore it down about twenty years ago, not long after they completed construction on the power plant. It had filled up with hookers during construction, which didn't make the city any too happy. So they condemned it and had it torn down. Beware the vengeance of the righteous!"

My alternative now is to walk to Oregon, five miles south of Byron on the Rock River.

After a pause, he asks, "Where have you been sleeping?"

I reply, "Since leaving Chicago, I've slept outside in my tent, alongside the road one night and in a couple different parks the other nights."

"Well, sleeping outside's not so bad, once you've slept on a steel slab in a prison cell."

Not wanting to go there, I thank him for the conversation and walk on. He gets back in his truck and drives off in the opposite direction.

The Gift of a Broken Heart

Jean is the innkeeper of the Patchwork Inn in Oregon, Illinois. She and her husband, Mike, restored the Federal-style building for that purpose. I am staying here for two nights to rest up before continuing on my way.

I am the only guest, so I have Jean's undivided attention. That is, she has mine. The morning after I arrived, she sits down with me after breakfast, and we begin talking. She tells me the building was constructed in the early 1840s as a private residence. A short time later, it became the town's first hotel. As it turns out, Abraham Lincoln stayed here.

We talk quite a lot about how Jean and her husband restored the property. She shows me a photo album documenting all their hard work. But we are soon talking about more private concerns, and at length about her divorce.

Jean begins, "My first husband and I had been childhood sweethearts. We began dating at twelve and got married right out of high school. We had two babies. He was a pretty unstable person, though. He died of cancer about a year ago. It's funny, I can't remember exactly when. It's like I'm free."

She got pregnant in high school. She explains, "Girls who got themselves in that situation in the late sixties either got married, went into hiding, had the baby and gave it up, or lived as single, sinful women. I got married."

I ask her what went wrong.

She replies, "My ex-husband left me soon after we got married. Though he hadn't been, he thought he might be drafted, so he enlisted in the army and was stationed in

Germany. I wrote him a letter saying that I wanted a divorce. He divorced me, then went missing for five years. It wasn't until President Ford pardoned all the draft dodgers and deserters that he returned with his German wife and their baby boy."

I ask, "How'd you live after he left you?"

She says, "The way I grew up, the bar scene didn't make any sense, so I was lonely. The Presbyterian church in which I grew up didn't know what to do with me. They didn't know how to treat me. It was cruel in a lot of ways. I knew couples who I had socialized with when I was married who wouldn't have anything to do with me after my divorce. I don't know if I or what it was threatened the women.

"I lived with my parents for six years before going back to school and becoming a nurse. One of my aunts owned a couple houses in Byron. I lived in one of them and paid rent of two hundred dollars a month. We didn't have much, but everything we had I paid for, and it was ours."

"I know what you mean," I reply. "As soon as my divorce papers were signed and sealed, I went out and bought my condo and set about making it my own. I've spent nearly four years painting and decorating it: making it into a refuge, as it were, from the stress of the city where I can live and be myself. What part of my heart I still felt without pain, I poured into that place."

Then I ask, "How did you meet Mike?"

"Mike and I met at church. I was attending the Church of Christ in Byron when Mike came to town to work as a welder when they were building the nuclear power plant. It was our minister who got us together. We met, started dating, and were married four months later. I was in my thirties. I knew my heart and didn't want to waste time."

She goes on, "Mike was a youth leader at the church. We were both dating other people when we first met. I wasn't all religousy at the time, though I had just begun a personal relationship with Christ and had let him into my heart. I decided to go to a bible study in order to nurture that relationship. Mike was in the same class. He knew a lot about the bible and had found comfort in it after his divorce. I'd become all steely because of all the pain and loneliness. Mike asked me out on a double date. At first I hesitated, but our minister really encouraged me to go. So I did. We had something to eat, went dancing, and I fell in love."

"That fast," I reply.

"I used to pray after my divorce. I'd pray for any man who had money and was kind of decent looking. Then my prayers changed, and I prayed for a Christian man who would love my children. And that's exactly what I got."

Jean asks me, "Why did you leave Minnesota?"

I tell her it was for a job and a chance at a new life with my now-ex-wife. "The job worked out, but the marriage didn't."

She shakes her head and says, "I don't know why you'd leave Minnesota. There's something about the water up there that draws me to it."

~~~~

A grassy courtyard stands next to the building. The grass is cool and green and thick. The courtyard is surrounded by flower beds filled with bee balm, black-eyed Susan, purple coneflowers, and tall sunflowers, among other native plants. The sound of bees buzzing fills the air.

~~~~

I lie in bed thinking about Michelle. It was in the wake of our divorce that I decided to walk to Minnesota. I no longer remember where I was or the time of day, but I do remember that the idea arrived with an irresistible certainty.

I imagined what it would feel like to walk out of my apartment, out the front door of the building, and down the street and keep going and going for days and weeks beneath a blue sky and across a green landscape. Until one day I would walk home again and everyone would be there, family and friends to welcome me back, to welcome me back home, safe and quiet, the quiet nights and deep sleep of home.

Michelle's grandmother painted glass eyes. She would be given a marble-like, glass sphere upon which, using the tiniest brushes, paint an eye that matched as closely as possible the one that had been lost.

Michelle's mother Diane grew up in a small town in central Wisconsin. When she was sixteen, her mother forced her out of the house claiming that she had seduced her husband, Diane's father. It had to have been the other way around.

Married and now living in Minneapolis, Diane's husband disappeared one night not long after Michelle's younger sister was born. When he returned some months later, he moved out his things, and they divorced. Michelle was two years old.

Thereafter, Michelle's primary contact with her father was his not showing up. And if he did, he either arrived late or left early. Once Michelle and her sister were excited that he was taking them to see a movie. A bar stood next to the theater. He left them in line and told them to get him when the movie was over. And then he walked into the bar. Michelle was not even ten years old. She was abandoned by her father over and over again.

Neither Diane nor Michelle ever wholly recovered their individuality and so they blended.

I of course had no idea of any of this when Michelle and I fell in love. But too soon thereafter we struggled to wrench her free of her mother. We never succeeded. Her mother won, and I lost.

I was no different than Michelle. I too had blended with someone. My heart was trapped in pain. Pain hidden in a darkness he had created. There was no room in my heart for Michelle. He won and she lost.

I played my part, enacting petty and destructive cruelties. And so, like many couples, we slowly drove each other apart, until one day it was all over.

I disappeared when Michelle left. And I was gone for a long time. I lived the first year in an apartment that I filled with portraits from secondhand stores, sharing my days with unblinking strangers. I kept the radio and television on and stopped listening to music. I stopped cooking. I stopped eating out. I stopped going out.

At any given moment, grief and sadness overwhelmed me as if I had slipped beneath the surface of a lake and slowly dropped beyond the reach of light and into the cold darkness that lay at its bottom.

Walking home one night, I felt my strength drain away, my limbs weaken, my breath shallow, until I stood motionless. I could go no farther. And the night rolled over me like a wave. I stood in the darkness, surrounded by illuminated apartment windows twinkling like iridescent sea creatures floating through the trees on either side of the street. Couples walked past, speaking in whispered intimacies. Everything around me was moving, but I could not take another step. I ached for love. Without it, I felt dead.

And then one day a couple years later, I woke up to myself again. I recognized once more the face of the man I had been shaving every morning, staring back at me in the mirror. I slowly made a life for myself in Chicago. But I did not forget the walk.

~~~~

Jean comes out as I am standing on the front porch getting ready to leave. I am spending the night at her daughter Dianne's house in Byron.

Before I step off the porch, Jean tells me a little story. "I can remember a time when both my children were teenagers and each had broken up with their sweethearts, and I had broken up with a boyfriend. I lay in my bed crying, and I could hear my children crying in theirs. I couldn't tell them that it was just puppy love and that they'd get over it, when I was feeling the same thing. So I went to my children and I told each of them, 'I know you don't want to live anymore, honey, but it will get better.'"

She gives me a hug. "I just want to tell you, Tim, before you leave, that there are a lot of broken people in the world. And that God gave you a gift. He gave you the gift of a broken heart."

Week Two

Oregon, IL to Mineral Point, WI

Remembering the Dead

Not far out of Oregon, facing west from the east bank of the
Rock River stands a monumental sculpture of an American
Indian by Laredo Taft. Taft intended it to celebrate the
cultural legacy of the first Americans, but over the years it
has come to represent Black Hawk, a chief among the Sauk
nation. Ironic that this towering figure should memorialize,
for those who benefited from his defeat, the last tribal leader
in Illinois to fight against the spread of white settlement.

Leading his people north up the Rock River, Black Hawk
fought American forces along an arc to the northwest ending
with a battle near the confluence of the Bad Axe and
Mississippi rivers. Standing before this towering figure, I
realize that my route north will roughly parallel theirs. I'll
cross the Mississippi just 10 miles to the south at Lansing,
Iowa.

I am leaving Illinois walking among memories forgotten
and undiscovered. Black Hawk and his people, failing to
regain the land of their memories, fled west into a future of
suffering and uncertainty.

~~~~

Further up the Rock River stands that nuclear power plant
the convict, who I met outside of Holcomb, spoke of the
other day. Enormous concrete buildings punctuated by
clouds of steam rising from cooling towers stand ominously
against the blue sky.

~~~~

Byron is a town of about three thousand people straddling the river one hundred miles northwest of Chicago. With time on my hands, I wander around and come upon an old Civil War memorial at the center of a residential intersection. It is an obelisk surrounded by a wrought-iron fence resting on a concrete pedestal. Two cast-iron navy guns, painted black and pointing south, flank its base.

It reminds me of the statue of Stonewall Jackson erected over his grave in Lexington, Virginia. He stands there in full uniform, hand resting on the hilt of his sword, looking north, with an attitude of perpetual defiance. And here, a bit to the west but aimed in his general direction, stand two guns of the Union Army poised everlastingly to crush any rebellion mounted against the Union.

The marble obelisk is weathered by years of rain and frost and difficult to read. In it are carved martial illustrations and a long list of local men and boys who had served. Most Civil War memorials in small Midwestern towns are made of granite and remain as smooth and polished as they did when erected over a hundred years ago. Like so many marble gravestones from the mid-nineteenth century, this must have been constructed sometime soon after the war, when the pain of all that carnage was still fresh in the hearts of the men who survived and the families of those who had died.

Standing there with a pack on my back, bearded, wearing dark sunglasses and a broad-brimmed hat, I attract curious looks from neighbors working in their yards, passersby in their cars who give me a wide berth as they drive around the monument, and a group of kids on bikes who circle wildly round and round, laughing and giggling as I read the names of those long dead.

~~~~

Dianne and her family live in a subdivision of Byron on the east side of the river. She takes care of the children while her husband works as an emergency room nurse in Rockford. He is working a night shift and will not be home until late.

My tent stands near an above-ground swimming pool covered with twigs and leaves. The kids keep an eye on me while they play in the backyard. They go inside, and I go to sleep.

North Grove Township, Ogle County, Illinois

There is a tavern in Forreston that looks like a church. Inside it is dark and cool: a haven from the sunshine and heat of the day. After lunch and a couple beers, I depart under the suspicious eyes of the bartender.

I call and leave a message with Marcella Ruthie, who runs the Evergreen Farm Inn. Needing to escape the sun again, I duck into an old Evangelical Lutheran church a couple blocks away. Inside it is cool, silent, and still. A stained-glass crucifix behind the altar bursts with golden sunlight. I lie down on a pew and fall fast asleep.

I sit up and look at my watch. I've been asleep for more than an hour. I take in the stillness of the sanctuary for a little longer. My mind empties out, but before I can do anything about it, he's there inside me once again. I shiver as I try to shake him off. He says nothing. And then he's gone.

An hour later, I am on the phone haggling with Marcella Ruthie, who finally agrees to drive into town to pick me up—for an additional ten dollars. I sit on the church steps until she arrives an hour or so later, pops open the trunk, tells me to put in my pack, and off we go.

Evergreen Farm Inn is a couple miles northeast of Forreston. And as Marcella explains, the farm has been in her family since 1845, after her mother's great-grandfather emigrated from Germany and bought the land from an "Englishman," meaning an English-speaking American.

We turn off the blacktop and down a gravel lane that must be about a mile long before reaching the farmstead.

The farmhouse is a large, two-story building with a welcoming front porch. The other buildings include a couple machine sheds, a barn, and a second house. The whole farmstead is nestled into the southwest flank of a small hill that is topped with tall white pine.

The interior of the house is decorated room by room and wall by wall with the accumulated possessions of five generations of a single family. Among B&Bs that try to capture a sense of the past with purchases from area garage sales, Evergreen Farm Inn stands out as one family's living history museum.

Though Marcella grew up on the farm and lived there during the first few years of her marriage, she spent most of her adult life in Florida, where she raised her daughters.

Her father inherited the farm from his father in-law and operated it as a feedlot for cattle. Each year was a cycle of birthing calves, planting and harvesting crops, and trucking cattle to Forreston, where they were loaded onto cattle cars and taken to Chicago's Union Stock Yards. She and her husband lived in the second house on the farm. They had two small children. Her husband ran the farm with his father-in-law.

It was the early 1950s. Many farmers in the Midwest still owned draft horses or mules. One morning, Marcella's husband, Bob, had left the house to harness up a team of mules to do some work in one of the pastures, when she heard a cry from the barn. Bob had been kicked in the chest by one of the mules. He died in her arms.

"We'd been married about five years and had two little girls. Judy was four years old, and Kathy was twenty-one months," she recalls. "He was twenty-four, and I had just turned twenty-five. I've always loved a challenge, but I wasn't sure I'd live through that one."

Marcella moved to Florida. She wanted nothing to do with the farm. But when her sister, who had never married and lived with their parents until their deaths, had died herself twenty years ago, Marcella returned to the area to see what was to be done with the property.

She found the farm in a terrible state of disrepair. And though she had not intended to move back to Illinois, she could not leave the farm in the condition it was in and somehow could not sell it, either. It had been in the family for more than 150 years, and selling did not seem like the right thing to do. So she and a nephew fixed it up, rented out the land to neighboring farmers, and turned the homestead into a B&B. She has run it ever since.

After talking for a while, I walk down the lane to a nearby church cemetery, where Marcella's family is buried. It is late in the day, and the sun is already nearing the horizon.

The graveyard is situated near an old brick church. It does not take long to find her parents, grandparents, great- and great-great grandparents, and other relations back to the mid-nineteenth century, all laid out and buried there beneath the grass and the fading light of the setting sun.

I sit down on the grass, surrounded by the history of European settlement in that little corner of rural America, resting on the graves of good Christian men and women, some of whom traveled halfway around the world to transform a strange country into the productive landscape that has raised and sustained their descendants right down to the present.

There was likely little room for doubt in the faith community that founded the North Grove Evangelical Church. Every step taken behind the plow, every seed planted and stalk of corn harvested manifested God's will. It was God's plan to civilize and make Christian the New World, including North Grove Township in Ogle County, Illinois.

They changed the landscape to see themselves as they had been in Europe, since all physical reminders of their former lives were lost across the Atlantic. Out of the word made flesh. They transmuted their ideas of themselves into the landscape I am now walking across.

With the past behind them, our immigrant ancestors created an America that reflected their zeal for Christianity, capitalism, and democracy. After the forced removal of the native peoples, the landscape was a blank sheet of paper upon which they inscribed their New Testament, America. And here I sit upon their graves dug into the landscape that still lives with the work they undertook to transform it. Their decayed bodies are at last part of the soil that nourishes those of us who follow.

But despite all the changes they made to the land, there still remains something of the millennia that preceded them in the wind, in the sky, in the land itself deep beneath our feet like an aquifer of memory, of knowing, of being that transcends individual experience.

The azure sky fades into black. Fireflies emerge from the cornfields, punctuating the gathering darkness with random points of light.

The Wind

Listening is transparent.

Listening is invisible.

What do we not see?

What do we not hear

That is transparent, invisible, and hidden?

~~~~

A few miles north of Shannon, a tall hill affords a broad view of the countryside in all directions. A group of farm buildings stands on either side of the road. There is no farmhouse. When the land was last sold, the farmer who bought it likely did not need the house and had it torn down.

As I stand there having a drink of water, up drives a sun-faded, orange Toyota pickup. It pulls off the road and drives up alongside me. An older guy wearing a red T-shirt gets out and walks over. He takes off his sunglasses and lets them hang from a string around his neck. Beneath them, he wears a pair of rose-colored, light-sensitive prescription glasses.

"You know, I seen you the other day east of Forreston and thought, 'What in the world is he doin'?' I wanted to stop then but didn't. I had business in town. But I kept thinking about it. 'Who'd be walking down the highway out here in the middle of nowhere?'"

He must be in his early sixties, lean, dark-skinned from the sun. His short gray hair has not been washed in a few days.

"Well, what are you doin'?" he asks.

So I tell him I am walking home to Minnesota to see my parents. "I live in Chicago now, but I was born down in Rantoul where Chanute Air Force Base used to be. We moved to Minnesota when I was a boy. We spent most of our vacations in Pontiac, where my mom and dad grew up. So I figure I'd just walk home. I've driven, flown, ridden a bus between here and Minnesota, but have never walked. It seems like a good idea to me."

He listens and looks at me through his tinted glasses. I try not to reveal the deeper reasons for my walk home, but he senses something. "You know, I was sick for a long time. My kidneys were no good. One failed, but the doctor said I could get by on one, and so I did. But then the other began to fail, and I was afraid that might just be it. The doctor said I could get a transplant and did I have any relatives who might be willing to donate a kidney. My folks have been dead for years, as are my two sisters. So I wasn't sure what I was goin' to do. And then my niece Sharon said she'd be happy to donate one of hers.

"And here I am feelin' a little better and a little stronger every day. I'm up to a mile on my treadmill."

He did not have much else to say. He shakes my hand and says goodbye, gets back in his truck and drives off.

What is it about walking home that makes people open up and share details of their lives that they ordinarily never tell a stranger?

The greater the distance I cover, the more I become a stranger. Like a priest sitting in the darkness of a confessional, sanctifying the telling of secrets, I am becoming the darkness inside us, the darkness that we speak to when we think we are speaking to ourselves. Yet the further I walk and the more time I spend in the company of strangers, the less I seem a stranger to myself.

Standing there on that hill with the landscape spread out before me, I close my eyes and feel the wind blow over me, around my body and across my face. I stand there with my eyes closed and feel just a little that the wind passes into me as well, and that in so doing stirs deeper secrets, making me feel both more whole and more aware of my own brokenness.

Time

At a bend in the road, an unusually large Italianate farmhouse towers into view. It stands on a broad lawn that is otherwise empty except for two large cedars and a weeping willow, like a nineteenth-century lithograph of a romantic pastoral setting.

The farmhouse has been maintained on the cheap. It was apparently built when the farmer was much more affluent than the building currently shows.

At one time it must have made quite an impression, what with its widow's walk, bric-a-brac, and wraparound porch. But much of its original decoration has long since fallen away. The widow's walk is missing, the porch's top and bottom rails are gone, and its original skirting has been replaced by diagonal lattice that is itself sagging in many places. Poverty strips away what's unnecessary for living.

To the left of the house stands an equally large barn in the same style. Most of the windows are missing. A flock of swallows flies in and out of the building, disappearing into darkness, returning into the light, disappearing into darkness, returning into the light, over and over and over again.

A little further down the road stands an old limestone, Greek Revival structure. I set down my pack, walk around the building, and find a faucet. The building looks in use. Perhaps it is a township hall?

A stone panel set in the wall above the entrance reads "Public School 1872." The windows are all shuttered and the door locked, so I cannot see inside. I stand in the grass in front of the building for a while and listen to the wind, the birds, and the insects. And then stand a little while longer.

I shift my weight from foot to foot, trying to give each a little rest. After being on the move all day, it is nice to stand still for a moment. All day long I have felt an irresistible need to keep moving, to minimize stops, not to linger long on any one thing, to pass across the landscape like an impression, like the wind or the light: be a moving thing and move along as all other living things move. I can feel my heart beating in my chest. I drink and feel the cool water fill my mouth and slip down my throat and into the darkness at the center of my body. Like the old stone building before me, I stand for just a moment unmoved by time. Time passes, intimating eternity.

Emerald Acres Campground

The Emerald Acres Campground office, dining hall, and recreational hall are all located in a large red barn. I step inside, set down my pack, and have a short talk with the woman behind the counter. She is in her late sixties: small, with a round face and gray hair done in a style more commonly worn thirty years ago. She, her husband, and one of their sons run the campground. It is open from the spring through the early fall, when they go south to Florida for the winter.

When I walked up from the road to the campground, I noticed that it was divided into two sections. The upper campground nearest to the entrance is empty, treeless, and without shade, and the lower campground is farther back, lying beneath a thick canopy of trees, full of RVs and campers surrounded by tall grass.

I ask about the people staying at the far end of the campground. She tells me that they arrive in spring and stay through the fall every year. They are either retirees or just people looking for the kind of work that moves with the seasons. The upper campground, where I have a spot for eighteen dollars, is reserved for short-term visitors, people camping out for a weekend or a week. I will be the only one here.

Much to my disappointment, the kitchen is closed. They only prepare food from Thursday night through Sunday. I ask about shower facilities, and she indicates that a small cinder block building across the way serves as both toilet and shower for the upper campground.

Outside, a few clouds begin to settle in; dusk is arriving a little earlier. Having set up camp, I grab my small towel and toiletries and walk the twenty or so yards to the shower barefoot, keeping a wary eye out for twigs and stones.

The building's metal door is so encrusted with rust and bent on its hinges that I have to squeeze past it to get inside. It is filthy. The roof is made of green, corrugated, translucent plastic. Large screened vents intended to let in fresh air and let out functional odors are set between the roof and the walls. But many of them are either ripped or missing. As a result, the building is full of insects, living and dead—mostly flies, spiders, and daddy longlegs—as well as leaves, twigs, and other detritus vegetable, animal, and mineral, as well as remnants of toilet paper, tissue, cans, and other items unmentionable.

I step back out. I am dirty, dusty, tired, and hungry. I do not want to climb into my sleeping bag like this. I take a deep breath, hobble back in, and do my best to get clean. I grab some errant pieces of paper out of the trash and brush out the shower stall and the toilet. Then I brush off the top corner of the door and hang up my clothes and towel. I step into the shower and spray it down with the rusty showerhead watching little insect and spider bodies flow down the drain. I quickly soap up and rinse off. I step out of the shower, which lacks door or curtain; grab the towel, careful not to pull down my clothes with it; dry off enough to get my clothes back on; and quickly step outside.

A car or two drive by while I am cooking, but no one stops or gives me a second look. At one point, the owners' son pulls up in an electric golf cart to see if I am the guy who walked in. He says it must be me, as there is not a car parked near the tent.

As night falls, the lights of the lower campground come on, shining out from the shadows beneath the trees. Though tempted to walk down to see if anyone wants to talk, I stay put and silently talk to myself. *This quiet that wells up inside me, this stillness that surrounds me, where does it come from? The further I walk, the less words are important. But in this stillness and silence, his words pursue me. Though I walk in the world, inside I run from the language of his lies.* I crawl into the tent and fall asleep before the first stars are visible in the night sky.

Alone

The rain began this morning in brief, mist-like showers. And then, as if the moisture was too great a burden for the clouds to bear, it came down in sheets. Now it is a deluge.

As I come down from the top of a high hill, lightning flashes above the clouds and thunder rolls across the landscape. The gravel road wells up into little rivulets, turning into sticky mud. I move from one side to the other looking for firm footing.

As I reach the main east-west route between Rockford and Galena, the roar of cars and trucks ripping along the rain-covered highway is deafening. I dash across and struggle up the narrow gravel shoulder, overwhelmed in a cloud of mist and grime.

Continuing north up another gravel road, stopping a moment to regain my equilibrium, I carry on, isolated in my rain gear, hunched over against the weather. Who lives in that group of white houses? One on a slight rise has a long, newly oiled, asphalt driveway. It glistens as sheets of rainwater pour across its jet-black surface. Two horses stand still in a pasture, stoically chewing on grass. A car drives by, and kicks up wet gravel and mud as it goes, moving across the road as if through snow, responding to the wind and the rain as it sways this way and that, accelerating and climbing the long incline.

A large burr oak stands at the top of the hill, silhouetted against the gray sky. I am on the road to heaven. I will climb up this tree and step into the clouds. I stand beneath the tree, pull off my hood, look up, and feel the rain fall on my upturned face. The rain falls steadily on the wet gravel, dull, plashing. A waterfall of sound surrounds me as the rain falls helter-skelter down millions of twelve-foot lengths of corn before dropping into the silence of the soil. Lightning flashes and thunder rolls across the prairie.

Paradise Cove

Ten more miles of muddy rain-soaked walking and I arrive in Winslow on the banks of the Pecatonica River just south of the Wisconsin border. It is locally famous for its artesian well. The town, which is no larger than 350 people, built a little park around it called Paradise Cove. People from the surrounding area drive in to fill up plastic containers with spring water. A donation box to help defray the cost of upkeep stands nearby. The park lies between a small limestone outcropping on the left and the bend of a stream on the right, beyond which lies the parking lot of a gas station and convenience store.

The natural spring cascades out of the limestone in a narrow stream of rushing water. The well at which people fill their water bottles is no more than a bundle of PVC pipes fastened to a wooden post. Water pours out of a faucet near the top of the post, where people can fill their bottles, and out of a pipe at its base. Both flow through another pipe set beneath the road and eventually into the stream.

I take off my shoes and socks, and gingerly put my tired feet into the rushing water at the base of the PVC pipe. It is icy cold.

It is a sad little park, not much more than a patchy garden of shade-tolerant annuals and some garden furniture that looks like it came from Menards. But what counts is that people want to make things nice—a doily on the top of a television set, a lamp made out of a statuette on a dresser, a vase with plastic flowers in the middle of a dining room table. We want to soften the corrosive effects of ordinariness or just plain ugliness. The town did its best with the resources available to it.

As I ponder all this, a boy rides up on a bicycle that is too big for him. The cigarette he is smoking seems disproportionately large in comparison to his small face. He does not look like he is much older than eleven or twelve.

"Hey what are you doing?" he asks.

I answer warily, "Well, I'm walking to Minnesota."

Hardly listening to me, he replies, "I moved here about a year ago with my mom. She works as a nurse in Freeport." He takes an awkward drag from his cigarette. "There isn't much to do in this town. My mom's gone a lot so I spend most of my time watching TV or riding around alone on my bike."

"Do you have any brothers and sisters?" I venture.

He replies distractedly, "Nope, just me."

"Where's your dad?"

"Don't know. He's not around. My mom doesn't talk about him much."

I avoid looking him straight in the eye. And though I can see he is trying to act tough, I sense his vulnerability. He stands a little precariously straddling the bicycle, trying to lean nonchalantly on the handlebars. He cocks his head to one side, then the other as he talks. He is just a boy pretending to be invulnerable.

His fingernails are dirty and his jeans smudged with grass stains. "There's nothing to do in this town," he goes on. "The other kids are no fun. So I pretty much keep to myself."

Despite the swagger, his eyes betray his loneliness. They betray the boy.

How I want to tell him his mother loves him and that he is a good boy, to scold him for smoking and for going about with such a dirty face and fingernails. His loneliness pierces my heart. I remember my adolescence. Trapped into believing a lie told by a liar; handing over my innocence for what I pretended to believe was love and concern.

Here I am, a stranger in town, engaged in a cross-country walk—what many think is a highly suspect activity—talking to a lonely boy in a secluded spot.

As he talks, I dry my feet and pull on my socks and shoes and get ready to go. "Well, it's been nice talking with you," I say as I hoist on my pack. "I've got to go now. Take care of yourself."

I walk across a small bridge over the stream and across the lawn to the gas station. I look back from the parking lot. He is gone.

Argyle, Wisconsin

After ten days and 180 miles on the road, the fertile plains of Illinois fall behind, and across the Wisconsin border lies the Driftless Area, through which the Mississippi River flows as it passes alongside Minnesota and Iowa on the west and Wisconsin and Illinois on the east.

Because this region was spared by the last glaciers, it retains an older landscape of narrow valleys or coulees, long ridgelines, and rock outcroppings. As a land apart, it did not figure into the plotting of territories and state lines and so exists almost in secret: the ancient homeland of a forgotten time, the remains of a world that no longer exists, lying partially buried beneath layers of glacial dust or drift and slowly revealing a little more of itself each spring in the runoff of streams and rivers flowing into the Mississippi as it in turn drains the continent into the waters of the Gulf.

Argyle, on the banks of the east branch of the Pecatonica River is a tidy community of about eight hundred people. A lumberyard and a couple machine and engine repair shops are located on the outskirts of town. Most of the houses are well kept and the storefronts in the business district occupied. There is also what appears to be an outfitting business near the river where people can rent fishing boats or canoes.

Though only on request, Partridge Hall offers the solitary room for rent in town. A former opera house, it now serves as a community hall and part-time restaurant. It took some convincing, but the owners finally let me stay.

I do not go into bars after dark. The chances of having a run-in with someone are much higher in a bar after dark than anywhere else. Someone's girlfriend gets too friendly as her drunken boy friend looks on. The next day, he drives up and runs me down. The farthest I can walk in a day is twenty to twenty-five miles. He can drive the same distance in fewer than thirty minutes.

Sorney's Bar and Grill offers up a dimly lit escape from the heat of the day. In the half-light inside, the bartender and two customers are watching a rerun of *Love Boat* on a television that hangs off the back wall.

The bartender puts down his cigarette and asks me what I want.

"An Old Style and a bag of chips, please."

He walks down the bar, opens a cooler and takes out a can, turns around and pulls a bag of chips from its clip, and sets them both down in front of me.

"Do you want a glass?"

"Yes, please."

The beer is cold and the chips salty. When the bartender notices my glass is empty, we exchange a nod. He sets another can down in front of me and takes away the first, giving it a little shake to make sure it is empty.

While I drink my beer and eat my chips, the three of them silently watch the television. They do not look like they are retired so they must be having a bump before going to work or going home.

The bartender shows some wear and tear. He is well into his sixties, yet with a full head of dark hair. His face is covered in salt-and-pepper stubble. And though he's slim, his breathing is a little shallow and labored. He is sipping a drink from a bar glass between drags on his cigarette. When *Love Boat* ends and *Three's Company* comes on, I leave a couple bills on the bar and walk back outside.

~~~~

I cannot sleep, kept awake by the creaking building and sounds from outside the open window. The ceiling hangs high above, barely visible in the dark. It feels more like sleeping in a banquet hall than in a bedroom.

The room feels like a dream. Has my life become a dream from which there is no waking? Was it an awakening that sent me on the road? Or am I falling more deeply into the dream I have lived all along? How long have I been asleep? Has this sleep become so large that I no longer walk in the world as others do, but in a cavernous sleep, a calcified dream of my own?

Walking. Walking. Every day I am walking. I awake each morning and all I can think of is walking. I open the door or crawl out from my tent. I see the road and begin walking.

The Mud Branch

Much of the wetland through which the Mud Branch flows has been tiled and drained off and is now under cultivation. Yet much is still swollen with watery meadows of muted greens punctuated by duckweed-covered and cattail-bordered pools of dark water, opaque beneath the pale light of the gray sky.

Where I stand, the well-maintained road is fairly wide and holds to the high ground. But the narrow asphalt surface of the road that runs down into the valley is cracked and broken by numberless freeze-and-thaw cycles and the high water table of the valley through which it travels. It offers the most direct route from Argyle to Mineral Point and must follow an old wagon road laid out by the first settlers, whose farms still cling to the sides of the valley.

One of them is a farmstead of red buildings trimmed in white crowded onto a small knoll on the gently sloping valley. Along the length of the barn are a large number of Dutch doors and paired windows set into a tall limestone foundation. A message painted on the side of the building reads "'Sjaahem'/The Nelson-Homestead/Dairy-Farm/H. L. Everson Prop."

Having grown up in southern Minnesota, I welcome this familiar message; it makes the morning feel a little bit like home. What does *Sjaahem* mean? Is it the name of the original settler? It sounds like a Norwegian name. Is it the name of the farm? That seems a little out of character, though. With few exceptions, midwestern farmers do not name their farms. And if they do, it is the Hank Knudson

Farm, the Michael Flannery Farm, or the Carl Schmidt Farm, simply identifying family ownership.

The habit of naming a farm is a bit too precious for the Midwest. The climate is too harsh, and those living on the land are too exposed to tolerate anything quite so poetic. Miles Davis once said, "In music, silence is more important than sound." This is true of whatever poetic quality there is to life in the rural Midwest. It exists in the absence of detail, or in the smallest of details intimately observed, or in broad, unbroken expanses of land, or in the enormity of the sky and the wind in your face. The simple act of working the land is poetry enough for most people.

Brewery Creek

The road cuts through the side of a small hill, leaving a bank of mowed grass running up to a fence that separates it from a grove of trees. It is a feature of an altered landscape usually seen only through the blur of speed. I lie down, look up to the hazy sky, and listen to the wind playing among the leaves behind me.

Further ahead, the road runs along the back of a large hill, making a long curve to the east. Open fields lie on either side. The wind rolls over the hill, and I hear the sound of bees. Hundreds of little bodies held aloft by a blur of tiny wings fly past and all around me. They ride the wind to the north, disappearing into the blue-gray light of the midday sun.

~~~~

In the valley of Brewery Creek
The air is thick with heat and humidity.
Crickets and grasshoppers chirp in the tall grass.
The trees whistle with birdsong.
A pair of turkey vultures wind circles 'round
Long columns of warm air in the hazy sky.
The sun stretches to the horizon,
Bending the light into golds and ambers.
Rising and falling,
The buzz and click of the cicada's song draws out
As if the earth were calling to the sun
To linger a little longer.

Local

Mineral Point is about twenty-five miles northwest of Argyle. It was named after the lead that was mined there in the early nineteenth century. It was one of the earliest towns in the area, established in 1827. The many limestone buildings create an atmosphere both ancient and primitive.

At a Lands End Outlet store on High Street, I buy a pair of purple flip-flops from a barrel of discounted footwear. As I look down at my happy feet, the bright purple reminds me of children's books filled with large-eyed, flowing-maned unicorns running through fairyland fantasy landscapes.

After two weeks of only hiking shoes, the soft cushions of the rubber soles are otherworldly. The open air on my blistered feet is life changing.

Because Mineral Point is a tourist town, though as yet not completely dependent on visitors, the commercial district is a mix of art galleries, antique shops, and boutiques as well as businesses serving the needs of the town and the surrounding countryside, including a hardware store, a couple of bars, insurance agents, law offices, and a drugstore.

The town is laid out along a series of ridges that rise out of the valley of Brewery Creek. The lead mines were cut into the rock on the opposite side of the creek from town, the earliest in 1825. The oldest parts of town were established nearest the creek. These older homes and commercial buildings were all constructed prior to 1850, largely made of local limestone along either Shake Rag Alley or Commerce Street. The homes along Shake Rag were restored in the mid-1930s, marking the beginning of the historic preservation movement in Wisconsin.

Though it is not uncommon to stumble upon early-nineteenth-century buildings along the major rivers of the upper Midwest, it is unusual to find them this far inland. Domestic and commercial buildings of the 1820s and 1830s are very rare.

Despite the buildings' small scale, the large, hand-hewn blocks of stone lend a degree of monumentality. In fact, when viewed in light of the time and conditions under which they were constructed, they seem almost miraculous.

Back then, they looked out on a native landscape that was still largely intact. Now, though the land and the hills remain, virtually everything and everyone else has changed. I walk up and touch one of the buildings, look up along its side, marvel at how plumb the walls are, catch the blue at the point where stone ends and sky opens up, and see in my mind's eye how the land might have looked to those who built it.

~~~~

Arkitekts Architectural Salvage & Gallery occupies an old creamery. The shop is divided into two parts: one disordered and dirty, filled with salvaged detail from torn-down homes and commercial buildings, and the other spacious and clean and arranged with old furniture, ceramics, and clothing—everything expressing a flowery, earth-toned, early-twentieth-century, kitschy aesthetic.

Arlene Byrne runs the shop.

"You must be the guy who walked into town," she says after I introduce myself. Evidently word has gotten around.

The store is empty, so we move outside and sit on a bench to enjoy the shade. I jump right in. "So how long have you been doing this?"

Happy to be asked and even happier to reply, she begins, "My husband Dick and I met in Chicago on the South Side, where we grew up. We were turned off by the whole obsession with money and status, so before you know it, we'd moved to Galena, you know, to get away from it all, and started a bed and breakfast. This was in the seventies before everything happened and the town was flooded with tourists. It was our secret. A place where we could live our own lives away from the mad rush for money. It didn't last long. They caught up with us, and now it's nothing but destination shopping. So we moved here to Mineral Point and went into the antiques business. Tourism doesn't bother us much anymore. We've gotten used to it, and we're old enough now not to invest too much in running away from, you know, that suburban, middle-class thing. It pays the rent."

"Where do you two live?" I ask.

"We live upstairs, though we still have a place in Galena."

"So what's the story with Mineral Point?" I ask.

She tells me that Mineral Point has been an artist community since the 1940s. The mining industry had long since played out, and the beginnings of historic preservation had established the groundwork for a new community of like-minded souls.

"You know, they say that two men, 'roommates,' restored the first building along Shake Rag in the 1930s. How many adult roommates do you know who restore an old building and turn it into a bed and breakfast and tearoom? Give me a break: those guys were gay. They always leave out the true story when it doesn't fit into their white, middle-class fantasy of what America is."

Artists and artisans influenced by the Regionalist movement of the first half of the twentieth century were soon establishing themselves in town. A second wave of artists and back-to-basics hippies arrived in the late sixties and early seventies. Mineral Point was perfect for them. Not only did it provide a lovely nineteenth-century ambiance within which to drop out, it was also cheap and relatively isolated: there was not a freeway for a hundred miles in any direction.

By the 1980s, there was a thriving community of artists, artisans, and writers pursuing the life of the imagination, largely ignored by and ignoring the wider world. To the extent possible, theirs were lives of their own making in a material world fashioned before machines, industry, and the resulting global markets had established their preeminence.

Arlene continues, "If there's a reason why we moved to Galena and then Mineral Point, that's it. We couldn't take it. Living in Chicago surrounded by factories, expressways, shopping malls, and people, people all running in place after the same thing. They were running after success or getting ahead, or whatever they thought it was. We were finished and got the hell out of there. And here we are. I'm sitting here talking to you, some guy who just came in off the road, taking a five-hundred-mile walk like it's as normal as the day is long. Not a bad life, is it?"

I ask Arlene about the locals. I had seen a couple bars along High and Commercial Streets that seemed to harbor the usual small-town alcoholics in their half-lit, smoky interiors—a far cry from the smoke-free, sunny, historically preserved tidiness and craft-brewed beers of the Brewery Creek Inn.

"I don't know a lot of the locals," she says. "We mostly hang out with the shop owners, artists, and craftspeople who live here. I have to admit that the town is divided between those of us who came here to get away and those who have always been here. When I think about it, I don't think they trust us, and we don't trust them, either. I mean, we've created our own local and have never felt welcome in theirs."

Mineral Point is not that much different from other tourist towns, where those who manage the trade are from much the same social class as those they cater to, and the locals are, well, local. How many of them are descended from those early Cornish miners who dug "badger holes" into the rock following veins of lead and later zinc, "mineral," as it was called in those days, and had simply stayed on long after the mineral had played out? How many were descended still from the German, Irish, and Scandinavian immigrants who had married local, raised families local, and stayed local for generations? How many had moved to Mineral Point from other towns in search of work or a chance to start over again, to create a new life from the unrealized hopes of a past lived elsewhere?

I straddle both worlds. Though I became an educated person, a traveler in the land of the upper middle class, and lived the life of an artist in Minneapolis before moving to Chicago, I was born local, from a family that was still predominantly local, and descended from people who had always been local. Do people like me fully pass from one demographic to another—do we become the demographic we currently live in, or are we forever caught in between, trying to make sense of a life we were unprepared for?

The teacher who abused me in high school promised he was shaping me to make this change, to become an educated person. He taught me about the history of ideas, philosophy, and psychology in the downstairs den of the split-level house he shared with his wife. He spent hours upon hours talking to me, and after each lecture he violated me on the carpeted floor in front of the fireplace. The person I am today is much the same person who spent so many hours in that lower-level room listening to and absorbing the thoughts and feelings of a man who in return extracted that vein of meaning we call ourselves.

I say goodbye to Arlene and go my way.

The Unplanned Can Be a Blessing

At the top of High Street stands a former auto dealership. Its red brick walls are in serious need of tuck-pointing; its wooden window frames in need of scraping, glazing, and paint.

But inside its dirty store windows are displayed hundreds of small found objects—pieces of wood, old tools, bottles, pieces of glass and broken ceramics, photographs, and large letterpress type. With a closer look, it becomes clear that, in many cases, the objects either have been attached to each other or are arranged in such a way as to reveal some purpose imagined by the person who dressed the windows. The interior is hung with dozens, if not hundreds, of Navajo weavings and crazy quilts.

It is dark inside. The only light source comes from a skylight somewhere in the back. Taped to the door is a business card. It reads, "Jamie Ross' High Point Arts: Continuing exhibitions visible through front show windows focused on: Photography & Typography, Assemblage, Concrete Poetry, Unusual Ethnic Art, Textiles, Visual Art with Words & Letters. Open Irregularly to Congenial Enthusiasts by Appointment."

I knock, then try the door. It is open. I stick in my head and call out. "Excuse me. Is anyone home?" I step in and call out again, "Excuse me. I noticed all the quilts, weavings, and artwork and thought I'd see if anybody was around."

And with that, a small, old man steps out from behind a partition and, not so much looking at me as around me, asks what my business is.

I reply, "I just walked to Mineral Point and stumbled on your work space. I thought I'd like to meet the person behind it all, so I knocked."

I cannot tell if he is intrigued or flattered, but with a notably flat affect, he invites me to follow him to find a place to sit. He leads me into his labyrinth of crazy quilts and Navajo weavings hanging above piles of the same scattered about the floor. At the center he sits in an old recliner, next to a side table with a telephone and a pile of papers and magazines spilling over onto the floor. He gestures to me to sit down, and there in the pale light from the skylight we begin to talk.

I tell him a little about what I am doing, but he does not respond. He sits there looking around me, not saying anything. Embarrassed, I take a deep breath and ask the obvious. "So how did you come to live here and to collect all of this," waving my hand at everything around us.

And with that he begins thoughtfully, as if talking to himself. "The interesting thing to me about sort of all of this and how it came about is that it's really not something that was planned, but something that developed." More alert to my presence, he continues: "And, as with most things, what I started out to do was not really like it is now. It was much more conventional. I really had in mind that this place would be like a museum, and it would permit me to exhibit my collection, and particularly the Navajo weaving. And I say 'particularly' because when I got this place, I had over four hundred Navajo rugs and only two crazy quilts."

"Why did you start collecting Navajo weavings?" I ask.

"I got aware of Navajo weaving fairly gradually. I had all these Navajo rugs that my parents had bought that I grew up on, literally crawling around on them. As a result, they're imprinted in my design mind. Early in my life, I was very interested in pictures where there was a composition, where there was a ground on the bottom and a sky on the top. And though my parents' rugs were very abstract, they seemed to my young mind to reference landscapes or cityscapes. I learned then that what I wanted to do was create the same things."

He points to a weaving hanging nearby. "I'm looking at this red one with the zigzags all the time as I talk, and its irregularities. There isn't a single form in it that's exactly like the one that it's matched with. Looking at it reminds me of the idea of making mistakes and then instead of crumpling up the artwork and throwing it away, you stop and rethink and see some way to incorporate the mistake in what you're doing and use it as a blessing that has gotten you out of your rut."

He continues as if speaking in an internal monologue. "So I photographed some of my favorite irregular Navajo weavings and took them around to show people who were weavers and knew about weaving, to get their opinion on this question: 'Is this just a mistake?' I heard really terrible things that made me begin to think of this as a definite issue of racism and philistinism all lumped together. I heard people say: 'They're just doing it to get it done to sell it.' 'They don't go back when they make a mistake because they don't care.' And another thing I'd be told is, 'They're probably making mistakes like that because they're drinking while they work.' It was a common idea that American Indians have such a serious alcohol problem that anything sloppy they do is probably because they were drunk at the time.

"But anyway, I thought of a rug that started out with a series of big serrated diamonds and then it looked as though one of the diamonds ran into the side of the rug so it ended up with a flat side, and from that point on the whole rug got less and less symmetrical. So I thought I could look at this and say, 'Well, they started out with the intention of making a regular system of diamonds that would start at the bottom and finish at the top. And because they calculated wrong and ran into an edge, they abandoned that scheme and did something different.' So my question was: why not just fix it and do it the way you intended?

"I asked this question of somebody who actually was a Navajo, who worked all day in a Navajo rug gallery. I was in Scottsdale, Arizona, at a famous gallery, when I asked the owner this question: 'Why not just fix the error and complete the rug in the way it appeared it was intended?' He replied, 'Well, I'll let you talk to a Navajo about that and see what he thinks.' So he stepped into the back room and brought out his coworker, who he introduced to me as Jonathan. I introduced myself and asked him why the Navajo don't correct mistakes in their rugs: 'Why not fix your mistakes and do it like you originally intended rather than letting it go all haywire?' And my thought was it would actually be better. There was a long pause, and he said, 'We Navajo don't think like that.' And I said, 'Well, I guess in my society, people who are craftsmen who would be weaving a design, if they discovered that they started putting in the wrong color, they would stop and undo it and go back and do it right.' And again a long pause, and this time he said, 'We Navajo don't like to go back.'

"And I don't want to overemphasize one little remark, but it was an eye-opener. It was actually advice that I had gotten from other artists, from my teachers when I was in college and graduate school: 'Leave it and go on.' And one of the ways to do that is to convince yourself that it isn't wrong; it's just something else or something unplanned. And unplanned is not the same thing as wrong. Unplanned can actually be a blessing.

"It's much more interesting that it changes. An experienced weaver is going to know that this is a more interesting rug. This is a journey; this is the way it goes. I was actually beginning to fall in love with accident and coincidence."

"But why have so many if they're just piled up?" I ask.

"Yeah, yeah," he replies wearily. "I have to actually look back on my life and recognize that there certainly was a time when I was an artist making art, and I had some rugs in my house, but I didn't think about them. Then I got a divorce. I shouldn't put it in the subjective that way because it wasn't really my idea. My marriage broke up, and my wife walked out on me after twenty-four years of marriage, and that's a long time. I had figured that there wasn't anything wrong with our marriage that wouldn't be mendable. But my wife was not faithful. She actually, although I didn't know it at the time, was sleeping with her department chairman. So it's like a smart career move, you know. And she became an administrator and moved to the central campus in Madison. By the time I retired, she was making about three times my salary."

As part of the divorce settlement, he explains, she wanted half of the rugs. "These were not just things to me with a dollar value; they were symbolic of personal discoveries; they were rare and beautiful to me," he says. "I love them."

He laughs. "Anyway, I didn't have to part with any of the Navajo rugs because they had come to me and into the marriage from my parents' estate."

I nod.

"That immediately made me value everything I got from my parents much more than I had previously," he says, looking at me intently. "I previously thought of the things that I got from them as just some old stuff that I didn't have a choice in, you know what I mean? It was just what they had. Whereas the things that I created or found myself were my own. But in fact, it was the other way around. Having lost half of everything I had collected during our marriage was a big stimulus to get more. And there were actually spaces on the floor that I needed a rug for."

The telephone rings, and he walks away to take the call. When he returns, I say, "I can't help but notice that there appear to be far more crazy quilts here than Navajo weaving. How did you come to collect them?"

He begins by explaining that he noticed crazy quilts at flea markets were priced much lower than more conventional quilts. And then after examining them more closely with the trained eye of a visual artist and professor of art, he realized that their aesthetic value far exceeded their market price, and he began collecting them almost obsessively.

He says, "I first noticed crazy quilts at flea markets in the area and began collecting them after my divorce. After I had been seeing quilts now and then, and thinking I can't afford them, I asked the price of one that caught my liking, and I was told that it was just seventy-five dollars. It was a crazy quilt. This was a third or a quarter of what I thought the price ought to be. It looked good. I didn't see anything wrong with it. I asked the guy, a dealer that I knew, I said, 'How come this is so cheap?' And he said, 'We resell things that we buy, and I didn't pay much for it in the first place.' The next time I ran across a quilt that I liked, that turned out to be shamefully cheap, I could tell that it was all hand made. Every piece was cut out and stitched together by hand. It must have taken months, and here it is for seventy-five dollars. The people who had them, that were selling them, that hadn't made them, didn't understand the aesthetic behind them. They actually thought that it's called *crazy* because there's no sense to it. You know, it's an irrational quilt.

"Well, one of the things I'd studied about aesthetics was how you have to separate the words that are used to talk about the thing from the thing itself and recognize that the choice of words is more than just factual meaning, that it has to do with values and feelings about things. And to most of these people, *crazy* is bad. I'm reminded of jokes: 'Anybody that would go to a psychiatrist ought to have his head examined.' But the idea that crazy people have something wrong with their head is really prevalent. So people made this funny association that a crazy quilt has something to do with the mood or the spirit of the maker being wild or out of control.

"But as I'm looking at it, I'm thinking 'abstract art.' I'd ask myself, 'How did they ever manage to do such good work when there wasn't such a thing yet?' You know, most of these quilts were made before abstraction had become a movement in fine art. That's what got me, because I'm looking at them, and I'm thinking Kandinsky and any of the other abstract artists who were arranging shapes to make a composition. It was perfectly obvious to me that the crazy quilt makers were doing that, too."

He points to a quilt hanging from the ceiling and continues: "This one, you can figure this piece that's right in the center is probably what they started with. They cut this rectangular piece and went from there one at a time. It wouldn't necessarily have been conceived with any kind of a plan, but each piece put in would have been an aesthetic decision.

"Well, I figure, looking at these things, that there just is no question that the person who is making it loves it. They love to do the work. They wouldn't be doing it if they didn't get a charge out of it. They're rewarded by what their eye gives them when they've done something. And that's how they know to go ahead. And I'm assuming this because this is how I make art, you know. If I've done it right, I really like what I've done, and I have the feeling that it's done right, everything is . . . I wouldn't want to change a thing."

He pauses for a moment then goes on. "But I also have to say that the women who made these quilts not only loved making them; they made them to make their lives and the lives of those they loved a little more beautiful.

"Looking back on the period that started when my wife left me and ended with my having hundreds of Navajo weavings and crazy quilts, I realize the significance of their all being women's work. They were made by women and made in order to keep their loved ones warm. They're made to go over a bed or wrap around you. So that the way I put them up here, it's definitely an enclosure in which I'm surrounded by loving female presences. It's not just a bunch of stitches or a lot of work; it's actually an expression of the weaver's soul."

And with that, he thanks me for the conversation and invites me to leave.

Although I plotted my route, walking has taken me to places I had not planned for—stitching them together by accident and chance.

Our brokenness is in our hearts, the source of our humanity.

It is already dark. I go my way into the warm night.

Week Three

Mineral Point, WI to Lansing, IA

Silence

The horizon rises and falls in great swells of earth.
The north wind scatters the clouds that obscure the sky,
Silver-edged islands of gray
Buoyant in a sea of blue.

~~~~

Twenty miles north of Mineral Point, I walk down into the valley of Harker Creek. It is crisscrossed by barbed wire fences and strewn with rusting farm machinery. A small herd of Holsteins lounge in the shade beneath the trees along the eastern side of the valley. But in the morning light, softened by the wooded, steep-sided narrow slice of sky above, the green grass and yellow wildflowers that overhang the sandy banks and stony bottom of Harker Creek seem almost a part of a lost or at least forgotten slice of time populated only by those who live nearby: a passing herd of deer at dawn, a pair of turkey vultures riding thermals thrown up by the mid-afternoon sun, or the nocturnal wide-eyed watchfulness of an owl, motionless as it surveys the valley floor, attentive to any movement that might betray its prey.

A cow moos and I walk on.

~~~~

The doors are unlocked at St. Phillip the Apostle Catholic Church in Highland. Gothic, built in the 1860s of local limestone, it is much larger than the more common

Protestant Greek Revival churches. The sanctuary is large, expansive, and unobstructed by columns. The stained-glass windows feature episodes from the lives of the Holy Family and the Saints. Each is dedicated to a devout and affluent family from the area. Beyond the chancel, the door to the sacristy is open. A large wooden cabinet lines a wall holding vestments and other items used during the mass. Its doors too are unlocked. The vestments smell of cologne. The fabrics are soft. I feel the raised needlework of the embroidery and imagine the passing of the liturgical calendar in the changing colors and decoration. A faint smell of incense pervades the room. It has a small sink with a mirror hanging on the wall above. I look at myself for a long time. My beard is getting thicker, and my hair lies flat and matted on my head. I look tired and worn out.

In the sanctuary is a small chapel to the Virgin Mary. I light a candle and bless myself with holy water.

At one of the darker moments after my divorce, I was talking to my mother on the telephone. I told her that when I looked in the mirror, I didn't recognize myself anymore. She responded, "I looked in the mirror the other day, and saw this old woman looking out at me. I thought, 'who is that old woman?' I feel the same inside, but I barely recognize myself anymore." She laughed.

I smile, kneel, and say a short prayer for the young mother above me, then walk back outside, feeling a little guilty for not dropping a coin in the donation box.

I set up my tent alongside the church. After eating, I sit on the grass and watch the light fade into twilight. Most people have gone indoors to eat dinner or watch television. Close to the limestone blocks of the church's exterior the air is cool. The breeze whispers through the tangled limbs of the pine trees above me and smells faintly of resin. As twilight falls into darkness, I sit embodied by the deepening silence.

Irish Hollow

It is the morning of August 30. Not long from now kids will be going back to school and life will return to the more measurably productive months of the year. The households across the street from the church rise and prepare for the day. Showers pour down hot water on sleepy heads. Husbands and wives ready themselves for work and their kids for day care, or their grandparents, or an outing to the local park. Televisions broadcast the morning news. The local AM radio station enumerates the Ag report: "At this hour, Barrows and gilts on the Chicago Mercantile Exchange are at $70.89."

Breakfast is on the table, kisses, and they enter the new day.

~~~~

As the pavement breaks up and returns to gravel, the road drops suddenly down a steep incline and into Irish Hollow. The valley's wooded sides gather in more narrowly. Though the sun is already high in the sky, the night lingers here. On the other side of a broken-down barbed wire fence, Holstein cows graze among the tangle of moss-covered trees. One walks up to the fence to take in my scent through large, moist nostrils.

At the bottom of the hollow, the gravel turns to sand. The crunch of footsteps along the gravel road drowns out most sounds. But sand is an entirely different story. I can hear everything as I move along, each step hushed by the sand beneath my feet. Behind the cries and songs of birds, or the diesel engine of a truck or tractor somewhere in the distance, the landscape murmurs to itself as the breeze rustles the leaves of the trees and passes over the crops in the fields.

The trees alongside the road change from oaks and maples with the strength to crack through rocky soils in search of water to poplars, aspens, and willows with expansive root systems extending out in shallow webs, drawing life from the damp soil like a fish's gills draw oxygen from the water.

Irish Hollow is a drowsy, almost enchanted place whose silence endows the air with a lethargy that is nearly irresistible. I fight the urge to stay. Twenty miles of road lie ahead to Boscobel, along the Wisconsin River.

Water, Please

After walking sixteen miles, I arrive at the valley of the Fennimore Fork of the Blue River where it winds to the northwest. The road runs alongside fields of corn and soybeans and past widely spaced farms. Where the valley wraps around the blunt edge of a ridge, it widens, then settles into open pastures and wetlands where the Fennimore Fork joins another stream.

A farmhouse stands on a slight rise above the wetlands at the base of the ridge. A man gets into a car, leaving behind a young boy in the front yard. My water bottles are empty. The boy disappears around the back of the house. I cautiously walk up the gravel drive and call out, "Hello!"

He comes out from the back and looks at me suspiciously.

The man who drove off must be his father. I hold up an empty water bottle and ask, "Is your mom home? I need to fill my water bottles and am wondering if you have a faucet on the outside of the house."

"She's not home."

He cannot be much older than ten. He wears blue jeans and a T-shirt. He is a little wary of me, but I think I am more nervous than he is. A boy at home alone with a stranger, a strange man. So I just repeat my request for water. He shows me the faucet at the back of the house. I fill up my water bottles, and with a thank-you and goodbye, I quickly walk down the drive and back onto the road.

Why am I so afraid to be alone with young boys? Who or what kind of man am I afraid of being mistaken for?

I don't talk about what happened to me. It's not safe. It stops everything. I disappear into people's fear and disgust. I'm dirty. I'm no longer the same person they thought they knew. They turn away.

Shame enfolds me as I walk down the road.

I'm running. I've been running for years. I carry this secret and fear the darkness that he unleashed inside of me. I run and don't look back.

~~~~

Like a dead coral in a living reef,
A leafless maple stands still
Unmoved by the currents of
The emerald sea.

Strays

It is very hot. There is no shade. The bright glare of the sun and the heat rising and falling in waves liquefies the landscape. I lose sense of my steps and myself.

I hear the sound of water splashing across stones. It is coming from the shade beneath the trees to the right. On the other side of a rusted barbed wire fence a tiny spring flows from the ridge above, splashing across a tumble of stones before it disappears in the shallow ditch alongside the road. I can almost taste the cold water.

Just then a car pulls up. A young woman behind the wheel reaches over and rolls down the passenger-side window.

"Hey, have you seen a small dog?" she asks.

A little surprised, I answer, "No."

"Well, if you do," she replies, "I live just up the road a little ways."

She notices my getup and asks what I am doing. When I tell her that I am walking home to Minnesota, she volunteers her front porch if I need a break from the heat and a cool place to rest for a while. "I live in an Amish log cabin. You can't miss it. I'm on the left-hand side of the road about a mile ahead."

Then off she goes in a cloud of dust.

Before long I am knocking on her door. She answers accompanied by three or four barking dogs, and as my eyes adjust to the dim light inside, I see more than a few cats hanging back, sitting on the furniture.

I take off my pack, and she welcomes me in. "I have this habit of adopting strays. My boyfriend thinks I'm crazy, but I can't help myself. I just love animals."

She introduces herself. "I'm Amy. Amy Olson."

"I'm Tim Herwig."

She looks to be in her mid-twenties, with brown, shoulder-length hair, a pretty face, and a friendly smile.

"Where did you say you were from?" she asks.

I reply, "Well, I live in Chicago, but grew up in Minnesota: Albert Lea, actually. I lived in Minneapolis for about twenty years before moving to Chicago."

She replies at length. "I've lived in the area all my life except for going to college at UW-Stout. I'm an RN. I work in Boscobel. It's only about a fifteen-minute drive from here. I don't think I could live anywhere as big as Chicago: too noisy, too much traffic, and too much pollution. I love it out here. It's so quiet. And I can have all my animals and not have to worry about bothering anyone."

She continues, "Out back I've got a couple horses and some goats. Let me take you out there, and I'll show them to you."

I reply, "No, thank you, just now. I need to get myself something to eat. I've got some food in my pack. And if I can fill up my water bottles, I'll step back out on the front porch and sit for a while."

Just then her cell phone rings, and, gesturing to the kitchen sink, she turns and begins speaking, I guess, to her boyfriend.

I eat my lunch on the front porch. It is nice to sit down for a while. I nibble on a power bar and some trail mix and drink a lot of water. Once finished, I step back inside and call out to Amy.

I ask her, "You said this was an Amish house? I've never heard of one."

Stepping out from the kitchen to meet me, she says, "You haven't? Well, I didn't have it built. It was built by the couple that sold it to me. But I had been looking for one. I wanted to live in a log house, and I knew that the Amish ones were affordable."

I reply, "So how does it work? They can't drive or use power tools, can they?"

"They, the Amish that is, prefabricate all the building materials off-site. They must do everything by hand. I think in Ohio. Then they have them shipped by truck to the building location, where a local contractor constructs the home."

She still wants to show me her horses and the tiny stream that flows behind her house, so we step outside with the dogs before us in a rush of wagging tails.

Her two horses came from owners who no longer wanted them because they were too old. Both show some gray in their faces and have pronounced downward curves to their backs. They both seem very happy and pleased by my brief visit.

We walk over to the small stream that flows behind her house. While she chats away about how much she loves spending time along its grassy banks, I am mesmerized by the cheerful sounds of the water, the play of light across its rippled surface, the rich browns, golds, and ambers of the stones and sand that lie beneath, and the fallen leaves that float by, wet and glistening in the sunshine. I am nearly overcome; a cool breeze crosses my lips with the slightest hint of autumn. I pull back, and the moment passes.

I am again aware of Amy talking. "I think I'm at that point in my life where I'm still figuring out who I am and what it is that I really want to do. I know certain things, like that I want to live in the country, to own my own home, to live with my animals and be close to my family."

Then she pauses long enough to look down at the stream. She pushes back her hair, and looks at me again and asks, "So, Tim, what are you doing? Why did you decide to do this, to walk home, as you say you're doing? What's that really all about? Are you trying to find yourself or something?"

I think for a moment and say, "Finding yourself, whatever that's supposed to mean, really is just the beginning. It's like writing a book. You finish that first draft and then you have to rewrite it over and over again to discover what it has to say, and then say it." I pause. One of the dogs walks up, and I lean down to pet it.

"I thought I knew what I was doing when I left Chicago, but now I'm not so sure. What I do know though is that something is happening. Something is happening that I didn't expect." Taking the risk, I tell her. "When I was in high school a teacher did something terrible to me. And when it was going on, and it went on for a long time, it was as if time stopped. I try to outrun him, but he's so completely inside me that up until now it's been impossible to escape. Now, though, as I walk home, slowly and deliberately across this enormous landscape, I realize that running away, of course, is not the answer. At some point, I'll turn to face him, and then... Well then I think I'll discover what I need to know."

I stop talking. The only thing that passes between us is the sound of the stream.

Crowley Spring

Morning arrives in Boscobel blanketed in fog. The hotel's red neon "Office" sign glows eerily. I walk up onto the shoulder of the highway and am swallowed up by the gray mist that, overflowing the banks of the Wisconsin River, has engulfed the surrounding bottomlands like a springtime flood. Headlights appear through the mist. A towering blue semi slowly motors by as if it were an oceangoing vessel and I a castaway adrift on a solitary raft.

~~~~

Posted at the entrance to a small roadside rest stop, a weathered sign reads, "To Crawford County from James and Francis Crowley, in appreciation for all the good things the Lord gave to them."

A gravel drive crosses over a culvert through which a small stream flows and leads to a picnic table beneath a wooden shelter. I sling off my pack, take off my shoes and socks, and walk gingerly up the grassy bank behind the shelter and sit down. A broken-down barbed wire fence marks off the little park from the woods that surround it. There appears to be an opening in the woods to the right. Just beyond the fence lies a large spring, rising up from the limestone base of the ridge above.

It is about the size of an above ground swimming pool. Overhung by branches and surrounded by bushy undergrowth, the spring is filled with fallen tree limbs, green water plants, and bubbling gray sands where the flowing waters spring up from the cracked layers of porous limestone below.

The sand suspended in the water rises like little spouts of snow from deep in the ground, where an ancient winter held captive in the rock for millennia is slowly escaping. Melting into waters that well up for a moment among the fallen tree limbs, winter overflows into a stream, passing out from the shadows beneath the hills and under the summer sun once again.

The stream cuts a deep channel as it flows toward the valley floor. A patch of jewelweed, still holding onto a few orange and yellow blossoms, lines the stream. The slightest touch sets them in motion. I stand above the stream, and the gravel and sand at its bottom disappear as its pale green translucence reflects the shifting interplay of sunlight and shadow filtering through the gently swaying trees above. As liquid silvers and grays slip from form into formlessness across the water's surface, the earth holds its breath and I see in myself the same shifting patterns of light and shadow. I look up and everything is quiet.

It does not matter that I am walking alone. I have made company with the land and the light that moves across it.

The quiet I no longer hear but now feel in my heart calls for a more courageous act. I stop running, turn, and look into the darkness to see what I can see.

Grace

"Bless us, O Lord, and these, Thy gifts, which we are about to receive from Thy bounty. Through Christ, our Lord. Amen."

~~~~

The rectory at St. Patrick's Catholic Church in Seneca, Wisconsin, is in an old brick house adjacent to the church. The interior is sparsely decorated with a few pieces of furniture and religious and rural-themed pictures on the walls. The walls look like they have not been painted in some time.

Sister Donna and Father Wolf have made a dinner of green beans, boiled potatoes, fresh tomatoes, slices of beef in gravy, and milk or water. Father offers wine, but it might be communion wine, so I decline. Though they are clearly on intimate terms, they address each other as Father Wolf and Sister Donna.

Before eating, we bless ourselves and say grace, they with a simplicity and sincerity so unlike the rushed pause before the chaotic mealtimes of my growing up.

We talk over supper and later over bowls of ice cream and homemade jellies about the church, southwestern Wisconsin, and our families. They listen attentively as I talk about my divorce and the events that precipitated my walk home.

Both of them grew up on farms and lived most of their lives in the area. Father Wolf, though somewhere in his late sixties, is still very fit, with strong arms and large hands. His thinning hair, combed over, shows little signs of graying.

Sister Donna has a sweet face and intelligent eyes and wears what seems to be a handmade lace blouse sewn in intricate and repeated designs. Both speak of their respective parish work, the deaths they have witnessed, marriages conducted, and baptisms. Years spent administering the sacraments to their parishioners, bearing witness to what is most sacred in life.

Father Wolf reflects, "My interest in the priesthood developed early, when I was a small boy and lived outside of La Crosse. My father supported my decision to enroll in the minor seminary. I completed my studies for the priesthood in Dubuque and was ordained in 1963."

He goes on. "My dad was a man of deep convictions and deeper faith. One winter Saturday night, a terrible blizzard blew in and shut down all the roads for miles around. At this point, we lived on a farm six miles from church; the parish was St. John the Baptist in Wilton; that's fourteen miles south of Tomah, in Monroe County.

"Dad got up the next morning, got the tractor, hitched up a trailer, then fastened a canvas over it. We all piled in and huddled together beneath the tarp to keep warm while he drove the tractor into the face of the blizzard six miles to church and six miles back. And though we were cramped, we were warm inside. All I could think about was my dad driving that tractor, peering through the wind-driven snow."

Though a man of few words, once started, Father Wolf talks steadily, moving from one subject to the next in a slow, thoughtful manner, peppered with wry anecdotes.

"For a time there in the early 1940s, my dad managed the farm for the Franciscan Sisters of Perpetual Adoration in La Crosse. We lived on the farm a couple miles outside of town across the highway from the Villa St. Joseph. So periodically some of us would go along with him to La

Crosse. A reporter for WKBH radio, at noon, I think, five days a week, would have a little segment they called 'The Man on the Street.' His radio name was Ken Allen. He would set up on the side of the Sears store in downtown La Crosse. Sears is no longer there. He had this little listening device up to his ear. When he got the signal, he would start interviewing people. Every conversation ended with an offer of a silver dollar if they could correctly answer a question. And a silver dollar was pretty big money in those days.

"So my dad walks up to him and starts talking. Ken gets around to asking him how many children he has, prepared to give us each a piece of candy. My dad answers, 'Well I have six boys and each one has two sisters.'

"The poor guy just stands there, and even I can tell he's trying to figure out how much candy he has to give. After what must have seemed like a long pause for the radio audience, my dad comes back with, 'that would be two and a half dozen children.'

"That was enough for Ken, and he reaches into his pocket and hands my dad a fistful of candy, and off we went."

Father Wolf arrived at St. Patrick's in 1981, and Sister Donna about nine years later. She had been working at a retreat center near Superior, Wisconsin, and had responded to a request from the Diocese of La Crosse for assistance in parish work. Forming a spiritual team, they each served a handful of parishes in the area. Sister Donna lived in the parish house in Wauzeka, a drive characterized by Father Wolf as "eighteen miles of hills, valleys, and curves with only two-tenths of a mile that is not a double yellow line."

I ask Sister Donna which she preferred working at, a retreat center or a small parish. After a moment she answers, "Oh, my. I've worked in parishes before where I was one of three, four, six, whatever, each of us having something of an avenue or an aspect to take care of. Here, because of the size of the parish, the location, the small number of priests around, it's like a lazy Susan: everything is on there; you do it all. And it may be that you don't find it out until it comes around: 'Oh, that too? Oh, that too!' But what's important is that we touch people's joy and excitement. We touch their pain and witness their disasters."

She pauses, then goes on. "Anyway, so that kind of thing is our story. I mean, we're part of people's lives. We may minister over the terrible death of a child in one family; then you'll have the baptism of a young mother's baby in another, and it will just be the highlight of her life. And you don't know. In a bigger city, where you have several parishes a person can attend, they can connect with several. Not here. I mean, there's one local corner where they kind of say . . . they don't use the word, but I think they think of it as 'That's the hub. That's the only place you can go. That's the connection.'"

At this point, Father Wolf chimes in. "The other day, a first for myself, we had a wedding of a young lady and her husband. And twenty-three years ago, I officiated at the wedding of her parents. Second generation now."

Sister Donna again: "You get to watch the paths families take through life."

Father Wolf replies, "I had the opportunity of presiding over that first wedding, and then a year later baptizing a cute little baby, and now that cute little baby has grown up to be a wife."

And after another brief pause, Sister Donna reflects, "You know I guess I look at all pastoral teams differently. Each is different from another. There couldn't be one like ours because there's only one of him and one of me. Ours is a deeply felt ministry to the church. I would have never thought I'd be doing this kind of work. It has opened up worlds. And I would never have planned this, although it's part of my background. It's what God prepared me for. So it's been a gift, really."

Father Wolf agrees. "These past fourteen years have been a blessing. Praying together with someone, to be able to share a prayer life and a ministry with Sister Donna, has been a blessing."

After supper, we walk over to the church to see the progress of a new renovation undertaken by Father Wolf and some volunteers from the parish.

According to Father Wolf, "it was built by parishioners in 1872 who clearly had only barns as models for its construction."

Very soon after it was completed, it began to lean to the south, so they secured it with rods and bolts attached to an adjacent grove of oak trees on the north side of the church. The sanctuary was first remodeled near the turn of the last century, again in the 1940s, and then in 1968. Vatican II had not been kind, and little was left of its original ornament except a group of statuary including the Virgin, St. Joseph, a crucified Christ—and a wonderfully kitschy St. Patrick outside just to the left of the front doors wearing a bright green costume with open-mouthed snakes at his feet.

But the latest effort looked to be a success: the old stained glass had been cleaned and glowed golden in the early evening light; the walls were freshly painted pale green, the ceiling white; there was lots of new woodwork, stripped and newly varnished pews, altar, and pedestals for the remaining statuary. The whole renovation had been designed at no cost by a local basketball coach who as a young man had dreamed of being an architect but had been talked out of it by his father.

We leave the church, and I tell Sister Donna that I plan to stay in Lansing, Iowa, for a couple days to rest-up before walking north into Minnesota.

She confides, "I think this long walk of yours, well, I think you're trying to re-create yourself in a sense. I think you want to come alive again. You know, Tim, you are alive. I hope this walk helps you find your way."

She reminds me to say my prayers. I tell her how my mother had always led us in a prayer to our guardian angels before leaving on trips. She thinks that is a good idea. "Remember, Tim, they do exist and often appear when least expected."

~~~~

After arranging some couch cushions and a couple children's play mats on the floor, I lie down in one of the parish center's activity rooms. The building creaks and keeps me awake.

The building has a Catholic institutional smell about it. A blend of incense and commercial cleaning products, damp carpets, musty catechismal texts, and the persistent odor of untold numbers of church meals and the accumulated perfume of the gray-haired women who presided over them.

Before turning off the lights, I catch a glimpse of a suspiciously blond Christ standing among a group of doe-eyed, multiracial children. It reminds me of the Sacred Heart Jesus that hung outside the kitchen in our house in Albert Lea. It was unsettling enough that the bloody image of Christ's heart was anatomically correct, but even more so that his eyes seemed to follow you wherever you went in the room.

One night, my brother Tom and I sneaked some cookies from the pantry. Downstairs we had to pass by a picture of

Jesus with his all-seeing eyes to get to them. There was just enough light shining in from the street lamp outside that we saw him watching us as we walked by.

Once we had found out where Mom had hidden the cookies this time, eaten enough but not so many that she would be able to tell (right!), and taken just one more each for the trip back up the stairs, I decided to perform a little experiment to find out how close I could get to Jesus before he saw me. Tom wanted nothing to do with it, and left me standing alone in the kitchen. I slowly sidled up next to the picture, then, leaning out from the wall just a little, I looked up and over to see Jesus staring right at me. I ran upstairs and jumped straight into bed.

Guardian Angels

It is September 1. The sky is completely clear for the first time since leaving Chicago two hundred and fifty miles to the southeast. After an hour north on the high ground, the road changes to gravel and meanders into the west, past farms and houses, down into hollows and up small hills, until it finally takes a sharp turn to the north, then into the west again, making its final descent into the shadows beneath the trees along a narrow arm of the valley of Copper Creek.

The air cools suddenly as the road curves to the left round the base of a rock outcropping dripping green and mossy with moisture. I walk right into a flock of swallows swirling in aerial arabesques no more than a few feet off the ground. I stop, and they quickly take to the sky and disappear above the trees.

The trees alongside the road begin to thin out, and the view to the left opens up to a fallow field of yellow-blooming goldenrod, purple aster, and clover punctuated nearest the road by clumps of green-leaved tiger lilies past their bloom. Further out are Queen Anne's lace, their delicate umbels curled up and gray with age, and a scattering of weirdly alien spiked mullein.

The road drops precipitously to the valley floor, and as it does, a ridge to my left falls away, revealing a broad, green meadow of close-cropped grass, grazing cattle, and the serpentine winding of Copper Creek bordered by cottonwood trees, willows, and random lines of quaking aspen. The bluff-lined valley stretches west into a haze, beyond which flows the Mississippi.

Some of the bluffs are marked by sandstone outcroppings. The greater the volume of water that flowed down these valleys when the Mississippi River watershed drained the last glaciers, the more pronounced the effect on the surrounding landscape. The ridges give way to bluffs made by great eddies of swirling waters heavy with ice and rock that ground out the limestone and sandstone formations into rounded promontories that now, worn and wooded by centuries of exposure to wind and rain, sunshine and snow, throw off thermals of warm air that turkey vultures ride in the heat of a summer day.

The Mississippi finally comes into view. The valley is nearly five miles across, with the river and its backwaters taking up more than three. On either side bluffs like great drifts of snow, rising more than four hundred feet from the valley floor, recede into the distance, one after another, disappearing into the haze of the late summer day. It takes less than five minutes to drive across the valley at seventy miles an hour, but an hour on foot.

The highway that runs north along the river shares the east bank with a railroad right-of-way. Both the highway and the railroad are heavy with traffic. The river valley that from a distance offered sublime vistas is in actuality a noisy and sometimes noxious arterial of commercial traffic.

The pack weighs heavy, my water is running low, and the sun shines down heat unrelentingly. I've already walked nearly fifteen miles. I have to stop, but there is no shade. Suddenly a decrepit Chevette appears out of the glare and pulls over. The passenger-side window comes down, and sitting there is Sister Donna with Father Wolf at the wheel.

She asks, "Do you need a ride?"

Without hesitation, I reply, "Yes!"

Sister Donna gets out and squeezes into the back, while I pile in my pack next to Father Wolf and climb in on top of it. And though the air conditioning hardly keeps up with the heat pouring in from the windshield, it feels wonderful to be off the road and moving ahead at speed.

In no time, a two-lane steel bridge, painted silver and gleaming in the sunshine, rises up ahead of us. We drive up the one side, across the main channel, then down the other and into Iowa. The ride takes just a few minutes, and I am standing outside the car in downtown Lansing.

I say, "What a stroke of luck that you drove up when you did. I was just about done in."

Sister Donna replies, "Was it really luck? Like many things, even our guardian angels appear when least expected. Good luck on the rest of your walk, Tim! God bless."

And with that, off they go.

Mount Hosmer

Lansing is situated along the southern shoulder of a large river bluff called Mount Hosmer, named after the nineteenth-century sculptor Harriet Hosmer, who during a stop on a trip up the river in the 1850s challenged a local man to a race up the bluff and won. Main Street rounds the southern base of the bluff, while the rest of the town either rises up its side or spreads out into the valley of Clear Creek where it flows into the river.

This town is only a few hundred miles from Chicago, but walking it means distance and time have taken me much farther. With so many days yet to go, it is as if I am on the other side of the world—thousands of miles away in a foreign country filled with strange people, my own thoughts held captive by a language no one understands. But here I am in Iowa with the Mississippi so close I can smell it.

Late in the afternoon, I walk down to the river. I sit on the embankment and watch as a series of barges lashed together and low in the water comes down the river, pushed along by a growling towboat.

Later still, I wander through town beneath the deepening blue of an impossibly clear evening sky pierced by the light of the first stars. Shadows gather in the wooded sides of the surrounding hills and bluffs. I find my way back to my room by the flickering lights of televisions and the blank-eyed stares of the people who sit before them.

The morning arrives bright and clear. I lie in bed and watch the play of light on the walls and ceiling as a breeze stirs the trees outside the windows. Lying there, I remember a dream I had last night.

After my family moved to Albert Lea, we drove two-lane highways each summer to my parents' hometown of Pontiac, Illinois. This was before the interstate was completed.

We are approaching the Mississippi when my dad pulls over in a dusty parking lot just above the river.

He says, "Kids, this is the Mighty Mississippi. It is the greatest river in America. It divides the nation into east and west and drains the center of the country into the Gulf of Mexico."

Without listening, my brothers Rick and Mark jump out of the car and disappear down the embankment above the river. Tom, Paul, and I follow. We leave Patty behind in the car. We reach Rick and Mark standing precariously on broken sections of concrete sidewalk trying to pee in the river. They fail. Tom tries and fails, too. Paul stands back.

The piled-up concrete looks too dangerous to climb on. I am afraid I will fall into the river. I hesitate, then scramble as close to the river as I can, climb up on a large slab, and pull out my penis. The air feels cool. Holding down my fly with one hand and myself with the other, I balance on the edge and pee. I did it. I peed into the Mighty Mississippi!

I turn around, and they are all gone. No one saw me.

I look back down the river, close my eyes, and imagine passing into the water. Swept up by the current, giving into its power, I am pushed carelessly forward, a boy alone at last and floating into the unknown.

Dad taps the horn, and I scramble back up the embankment and into the waiting car.

~~~~

The day is nearly over. As night approaches, I decide to walk up Mount Hosmer. The park at the top is empty. The picnic tables sit quietly beneath the trees. I stand alone at the edge of the cliff. The bluffs lining the Wisconsin side of the valley stretch as far to the north and south as the turning of the horizon allows.

Below, the steel bridge gleams silver in the light of the setting sun. Connecting the present and the past, it marks the geographic midpoint of a story whose ending remains beyond the setting sun.

The river stretches out before me. My body like the earth flows with water.

Week Four

Lansing, IA to Albert Lea, MN

The Valley of the Upper Iowa

The road follows a little rise and reveals fields of uniformly tall corn in row upon countless row stretching across the broad floodplain of the Upper Iowa River. Ahead stands a single, solitary hill covered with pine and hardwood trees. It is surrounded by fields of corn like a carefully selected stone placed on the raked sand of an enormous Zen garden.

~~~~

A well-tended farm stands on the high ground to the left of the road. There is road construction ahead. A teenage boy is working in the yard. I hold out an empty water bottle and ask, "Would you mind if I filled it up?" His dad comes out of a large machine shed wiping his hands on a dirty rag.

As they walk toward me, their feet unsettle a fine white dust that covers the grass. They each wear Red Wing work boots, blue jeans, white T-shirts (the dad's bearing a knockoff of Grant Wood's *American Gothic*), and billed caps, the boy's fashionably curled under, his dad's straight across. They both have powerful forearms like a Popeye cartoon.

They are happy to oblige my request and direct me to an outdoor faucet near the machine shed. They wait as I fill up both bottles.

We talk for a while. I ask them about the road construction and the dust.

The father replies, "The dust isn't the problem; it's that the county has decided to punch another road through our fields; that's the problem. They couldn't just widen the old one; they had to build a new one twice as wide as the first."

I ask why. He replies, "It used to be that roads were built either side of a valley. Here where the river flows east/west, the road was built on the north, as the sun is in the southern sky all winter. In that way the sun melts the snow and dries out the mud earlier in the spring, making the road passable sooner than if it was built on the south bank. If you build a road along the side of a valley and not across it, you leave more land free to farm."

~~~~

An old wrought-iron bridge crosses the river. The wooden plank deck is scattered with gravel kicked up by passing cars. A sign on an upright notes the bridge number and that it was forged in Chicago, like so much of the infrastructure of the Midwest from that time. The river is shallow and passes quickly by.

~~~~

Mount Hope Church stands above the north side of the valley. It is a sad little church clad in dirty white siding. Somewhere beneath there must be a nice mid-nineteenth-century building.

I sit down in the shade of a tall cedar and look out onto the small graveyard. After a while, I get up and have a look around.

There is a single father and son gravestone for Joseph and John Williamson: Joseph was born in Ireland in 1798 and died in 1878. His son John served in the Union cavalry in the Civil War and died in 1876 at the age of forty-four. Had he lived with his dad all those years and never married? And what were Joseph's last years like, living on after his son had died?

Then there is Mrs. Sarah Hammond, who was born in 1798, and Jacob Singleton, born in 1795, a veteran of the

War of 1812. Both stones were cut from white marble. Mrs. Hammond's is rectangular with an image of an open bible carved in relief above the inscription. Jacob Singleton's is an obelisk like a small chess piece. The lives of Jacob Singleton's wife and children are noted on the gravestone, but there is no sign of Mr. Hammond's grave. Either he was buried elsewhere or, like many markers made of marble, his had long ago been broken into fragments by the frost, dissolved in the rain and snow, and swallowed up by the earth.

Coming across graves of people born in the eighteenth century there on the shoulder of a river valley in northeastern Iowa makes this place seem even more remote from the present moment. What must they have seen that now is largely forgotten and almost entirely vanished from the landscape? Now all that is left of them is a gravestone that over time lists with the ebb and flow of the land from winter frost to springtime thaw, slowly eroding until the inscription marking its purpose is wiped clean. Like a pale ghost it hovers over the dark earth at twilight or all but disappears in winter, white against white, as if it had never been there. And then it is gone like the life it was placed there to mark.

I lie down in the aromatic shade beneath an ancient cedar and feel the almost imperceptible slowness by which the landscape changes, where a century is no more than a minute increment of time measured in millennia.

~~~~

An historical marker on the side of the road indicates that a feature up ahead is called "Elephant Hill." According to the marker, early settlers had used it to navigate the valley's twists and turns. The hill stands alone, dark green silhouetted against the bright blue sky. And after a while, the elephant slowly emerges like a 3-D image in the Sunday paper that suddenly appears as you relax your gaze and allow it to focus your attention. There it is, just as described, an elephant lying on its haunches with its trunk extended out in front, coalesced from indistinguishable elements to form a single image right out of a Rudyard Kipling story or from a colorful circus poster. Had I been driving, there would not have been time to recognize it. A farmer living in the mid-nineteenth century had plenty of time to imagine elephants.

~~~~

The road holds tight to the northern side of the valley. Because of the road construction there is no traffic. The quiet is liquid. Birds fly among the trees and over the fields like fish darting across aquatic grasses swaying in the sunlight within the slow-moving current of an enormous river.

Dorchester is five miles ahead. The heat of the late afternoon is intense. What water I have left is as warm as bathwater. Having left the valley behind, the highway begins to climb. It crosses a bridge high above a rocky stream. The road is busy with traffic traveling to and from the Iowa-Minnesota border.

The bridge has no shoulder. At a break in the traffic, I walk on as quickly as the sun and heat of the day will allow. The bridge cannot be much more than fifteen or twenty yards long. Ahead the highway climbs up and around the base of a ridge, then out of sight.

As I reach the midway point, not one but two semis come round the bend and bear down on me. Too confused to run ahead or back, I sit down on the concrete embankment at the side of the bridge, swing my feet over, and drop.

With a jolt, I land on an unseen ledge. A cow stands in the stream below looking up at me. The first truck roars by, and then the second. Shaken, I scramble back up and get off the bridge as quickly as possible.

Waterloo Workshop: Make a Life Not a Living

(Waterloo Workshop brochure)

Hand-woven 'Baskets-with-a-Purpose' Delicious Jams and Relishes made from wild and locally-grown Fruits and vegetables: carvings, woodenware, mirror, and picture frames.

In our old log home we live much as people used to 100 years ago, with no electricity or telephone. We continue to practice the old-time arts of wood-working, basket-weaving and preserving wild or home-grown fruits and vegetables.

Feel free to drop in anytime—we're almost always home. If you want to be sure, send us a note when you'll be here and we will too.

In addition, we invite folks into our home the 2nd Sunday of every month from 11 to 4, year round.

Visitors share fresh, made-from-scratch rolls baked in our wood stove, sample country jams and sip tea or fresh well water.

They partake of a good old-fashioned country visit, the way things used to be.

As the valley of Waterloo Creek rises, the ridgelines recede. Fog floats up from beneath the trees. Sunlight slowly opens in the sky, extending the half-light of dawn lazily into the morning.

I make my way out of the Driftless region along the winding course of the stream. Ahead lies Bee, Minnesota, on the border with Iowa. From there the prairie gradually opens up without disruption until the Rocky Mountains.

Round an easy curve, the gravel road passes right through the Waterloo Workshop. A log cabin and large garden are on the left; to the right, a woodworking shop and small grove of fruit trees.

Just as a scrappy Jack Russell terrier comes barking, a voice cries out, "Hey, Robert! Get back here! Here, Robert!"

A large man with long white hair and a longer gray beard looks up from a barn-sized wooden window frame with mallet in hand. He looks to be in his mid-seventies and wears a denim shirt with the sleeves rolled up and a pair of canvas shorts held around his substantial midsection by a drawstring. Robert backs off a little, but follows close behind.

"Hello. My name is Tim Herwig. Are you Michael Stephenson, and is this the Waterloo Workshop? I'm on my way to Albert Lea, Minnesota. I heard back in Dorchester that if I came up Waterloo Creek, I'd find you."

"Yes, I am Michael Stephenson, and this is the Waterloo Workshop," he replies, looking a little put out.

I begin to go on but see that the little I have said already is more than he wants to know. It appears the brochure I read last night was stating requirements and not recommendations about visits. It is not Sunday, and I did not write a note.

Despite seeing that he wants to get back to work, I ask him about the project. With undisguised weariness verging on exasperation, he explains that he is making a window frame for a barn door. "You can't buy a window for an old barn at a Menards or Home Depot," he says. "You have to make a new one. These old barns were all framed up by hand, and so every window and door is a little different from all the others. Standards of construction hadn't been established, so every building had its own character and peculiarities."

Having warmed up to me a little, he sets down his mallet and invites me around for a little tour of the place and to meet his wife, Jill, who is in the cabin. He points out his woodworking shop and the fruit trees they had planted surrounding it. It is a simple building with red-stained vertical siding, resting a little above the ground on concrete piers. Posted on the outside are a series of hand-painted signs reading "M. Stephenson Woodworker: Windows, Signs, Old Tools, and Doors." He must have built it himself.

The three of us—including Robert—walk across the road to their home. It is an old whitewashed log cabin made of squared-off timbers and concrete chinking. It appears to have a full second story, and at some point, the Stephensons must have built an entrance porch and small rear addition.

We duck inside, and Michael calls out, "Jill, we have a visitor."

Jill steps out from the back room and greets me with a friendly smile. Her recommendation—*send us a note*—appears to be his requirement. She and I sit down at a table in the middle of the room, and Michael sits a little apart in a rocking chair. Jill seems younger than Michael. Her hair has not turned gray so much as the original brown has faded out. She is about the same height as her husband, though much slimmer, and wears wire-rimmed glasses.

She offers me a bran muffin and a glass of water. She steps away for a moment, and I take a look around. Like the exterior, the walls are whitewashed. One side of the cabin serves as a kitchen and the other as an all-purpose living space. The walls are lined with furniture serving a variety of storage uses. In the kitchen area are wood and propane stoves, a sink, and a handful of small tables and open cabinets full of dishes, pots and pans, herbs and spices, bakery and other dry goods. The living area has a couple rocking chairs, a few more small tables, a battery-powered radio, and a highboy.

I ask myself, *How do people live in such a small space?*

Jill recognizes my unspoken question and explains, "It's actually pretty easy to live in a small space. In fact, this is actually pretty big for a log cabin. It had originally been used as a store down the valley in Dorchester. We don't know what kind of store; we assume a general store back in those days. And probably the family that ran it lived upstairs, which is the reason it's such a large house—for a log house built back in those days, that is. And then because they lived upstairs, the roof comes down to four-foot walls instead of right straight down to the floor. So there is a lot of extra space."

Warming up a little more, Michael decides it is time to tell their story. "We moved here in 1992 from Cary, Illinois. It's a suburb of Chicago. When we first moved there, it was a nice little farm town. It took you all morning to go to the bank because you knew everybody and had to stop and talk. When we left seventeen years later, it was three times the size and people were mean. A lady in a bank said it well: 'You know, all these people coming out here from Schaumburg to get away from that place, they don't realize that they're bringing a lot of it with them.' And they ran all the farmers out, sometimes in nasty ways, like building a subdivision of forty houses and draining all the water off the streets into the farmer's field across the road.

"It wasn't a typical suburban life, though. We were caretakers of the county conservation district—a 250-acre piece of land—and lived in an old farmhouse and practiced subsistence farming."

With a glint in his eyes, he adds, "Our two girls used to bring their friends over and peek around at the buildings and tell them that we were flower children."

"So, can you tell me about how you decided to live like this?" I ask. "I mean, is it just that this is what you could afford, or was there more to it than that?"

Michael begins: "We didn't look for electricity. We looked for a place to live. And this happened to be the one that we found that we could afford, that's all. In fact, we had found a place before. We even put earnest money down on a place, and through all kinds of shenanigans, we didn't get it. I think somebody stopped it."

"Well, I think cost was a big part of it," replies Jill as if she had not heard what Michael said. "That was certainly a limiting factor. I think we really liked the idea of living in an old house rather than having to build something new. We liked the idea of living without electricity, being more independent, and limiting our contribution to the problems our world is faced with. But it was kind of a gradual thing, I think. It wasn't a revelation: 'Oh, this is the way we want to live!' It was more of a gradual, 'Oh, this seems like a good idea.'

"One thing that became more apparent to me—and I don't know, maybe it was something that was apparent to Michael right from the beginning—there's a very satisfying feeling in knowing that you can take care of yourselves without having to rely on all the infrastructure of civilization.

"Knowing you can handle things in a more direct way; you can figure it out if there's a problem. You don't have to necessarily call the nearest repairman. It's the feeling of self-sufficiency, even though we aren't raising as many of our food crops and animals as we used to do back in Illinois."

"But self-sufficiency works best when you live among a community of people who respect that decision and treat you like family," Michael notes.

"I went to Spring Grove a couple weeks after we first moved here," he recalls. "The hardware store in town had a big fiberglass tub to mix concrete in for caulking things. I filled it up with tools that I needed to start working on the house. And I reached for my checkbook and said, 'Oh, I left my checkbook at home. Leave everything here. I'll come right back and pay.' The guy behind the counter says, 'No, you don't have to do that.' And he wrote me out an envelope with his address on it and said, 'Send me the check.' He had never seen me before. I couldn't believe it. I mean, think of where I came from: you had to pay for gas ahead of time, and some of the doctors wouldn't take a check for their payment. I mean, it was a revelation. I just never realized that people treated people like that."

Jill adds with the same mix of astonishment and gratitude, "And this kind of thing happened time and again after we first moved here. It was just incredible."

There is a pause long enough for the house's silence to settle in for a moment. Then Michael begins again. "The local family that made the biggest impression on me after we moved here were the Schultes, Theodore and Leonitas Schulte.

"When they got married in 1950, they decided not ever to buy anything they didn't have the money for, and so they didn't. And he said it was really bad for the first few years. They would literally put the machinery together with baling wire. Most people don't know what that is. They wore shoes that didn't match, and they did everything by themselves. They took care of everything, and they were very poor, because they didn't go out and buy stuff on credit like everybody else was doing.

"But then, not very far down the line, they realized they were buying things cheaper than everybody else because they never paid any interest on it. And when it came to the eighties and the banks were picking up all the land from farmers who had defaulted on their mortgages, he had the money to pay for land that was close by his that he wanted. So he'd buy the land from another farmer and give them an extra ten percent, so they had a little bit to start out someplace else again and the bank wouldn't just take it and leave them broke. I don't know how much money they have now, but they're well-to-do. You wouldn't know it to look at him, though. He drives a 1970 pickup truck, and his son fixes it up for him all the time. Is he ten years older than I am?"

Jill answers, "I think he's eighty-eight."

Michael continues, "And he works every day but Sunday. And she ran an egg route. She had two hundred chickens, and she'd sell to restaurants and stores and individuals. And she kept a very good garden, a big garden. They must have grown fifty bushels of potatoes every year.

"Leonitas died. That must have been seven or eight years ago now. He's still mourning her. They were very close."

Jill steps in again: "But before she died, she taught him how to cook because he had never cooked before in his life. He grew up in a family with all sisters, and he'd never had any need to cook. So she made a point of giving him cooking lessons so that he could cook for himself and the youngest son who farms with him. The son doesn't live in the same house but comes and has at least one meal a day with him. And she also filled the freezer with homemade pies and meals, trying to take care of him, even though she knew she was going to be gone soon. She also made all the funeral arrangements. She didn't want him to have to deal with that."

Michael again: "She ran the church. She played the organ, and she was the choir director, and she took care of the flowers and told the priest what he was supposed to do. She was a very good organizer and was also very kind. She was a really good neighbor. If anybody had a problem, she did what she could to help out."

Jill again: "And they raised seven children."

Michael, as if making a point about how difficult it is to raise children: "And the remarkable thing was that none of the kids turned out bad."

In agreement, Jill: "It's a good bunch."

Michael again, reinforcing his point: "They were just good working people. They weren't doctors or lawyers or politicians. None of them ended up in jail, and none of them was a drunk, and none of them was a murderer, and none of them was a deadbeat. And they're very nice people, and good friends.

"Leonitas didn't want people to feel bad about her dying, so she bought twenty-five copies of a book explaining about heaven. She gave one to Jill, too. She wanted people to know that it was okay, what she was going through, and they shouldn't worry about it. And this is not because she felt sorry for herself. I don't think she knew how to feel sorry for herself. She was really worried about other people. She was quite a woman."

I look at my watch and realize I have been here for over an hour. I have to get going.

"Thank you for the muffin and conversation. I've got to be on my way. I want to reach Spring Grove before it gets much later in the day."

Jill says, "You're very welcome. I'm afraid we didn't ask you about your walk. But then again, you seem determined, and so I trust you know what you're doing."

I step outside. Before returning to the road, I take a long drink of water. Clear, cool water flows into my mouth and down my throat. I listen. The sun is shining, and I listen a little longer. Jill and Michael kept talking, and I listened.

Trolls

Waterloo Creek flows beneath an old bridge on the south side of Bee, Minnesota. It is less a town than a group of derelict houses, cars, and farm equipment gathered round a gravel road. The buildings look like they have not been painted since the Depression. Just beyond the bridge is a small sign no more than four feet off the ground that reads, "Minnesota State Line." It has taken twenty-two days to walk three hundred miles from Chicago to Minnesota.

Why is this sign so low to the ground? It's almost as if it were intended for someone on foot and not in a car, I think to myself.

I suddenly feel that someone is standing behind me. I turn around, and right there is an old man in dirty work clothes and a cap that reads, "Boondocks, USA."

Standing there unsteadily, looking both menacing and confused, he squints in the sunlight as if he has just walked out of some dark place.

Why didn't I hear him? I ask myself.

We look at each other in silence, until finally I venture, "Hello!"

He does not say anything.

He takes a step closer, and I turn around and walk quickly away.

~ ~ ~ ~

The road takes a steep little rise out of town, the valley falls behind, the sky opens up, and the land rolls on into the west. I feel the wind on my face for the first time in days. Everything is movement and sound.

I turn my head to the side, and what I thought was the sound of the wind falls away. I take a deep breath, and my pack creaks a little. The wind makes no noise; it gives voice to everything it passes over.

~~~~

Spring Grove, Minnesota is a tidy little place. It claims to be the first Norwegian settlement in the state. At some point, the cemetery's scattering of old gravestones disturbed the community's leaders, so they pulled them all up and cemented them into two neat rows at the back and made a park out of what remained.

Downtown has a lot of secondhand stores. I'm drawn across the street to a combined antique store and Laundromat. Once inside, I'm assaulted by terrible screaming, like the desperate cries of an animal whose life is being squeezed out of it.

Looking up, I see the ceiling is completely covered with stuffed animals and dolls. There must be thousands of them of different colors, sizes, and shapes, each nailed by the neck to the ceiling.

At the back of the Laundromat, beneath the blank stares of impaled dollies and doe-eyed stuffed animals, stands a little boy with his back to me. He is looking down on a crouched, wiry, middle-aged man holding down a small cat fighting like crazy to get away. It had pissed all over the floor.

I yell out, "What are you doing?"

He replies, "It didn't piss on my shoes did it?"

I indicate that it hadn't.

Yelling over the screaming cat: "I trap feral cats, tame them, and give them away. It's a lot easier to tame four legged than two legged. You can predict what a four-legged animal will do, but not a two-legged one."

He sees the distress on my face and goes on. "Don't worry; I'm not hurting it. The kittens struggle like this for fifteen minutes; adult cats for thirty. Then they quiet down."

Even though he does not appear interested, I introduce myself. "My name is Tim Herwig. I'm on my way to Albert Lea. I'm walking."

Apparently catching only my name, he yells over the sound of the still-struggling cat, "Everybody calls me Lucky. You can just call me that if you want to call me anything. Standing there is my grandson." The stunned child looks on without expression.

Eventually, the cat calms down. Lucky returns it to its cage. The Laundromat is quiet except for a couple running washers and dryers.

"What's going on with all the dolls and stuffed animals," I ask, waving my hand in the air.

He says, "It's just something I started and can't stop. There's 2,637 of them."

I ask, "How did all this happen?"

He replies, "Why do people collect anything? One guy comes in here collects girdles. Everybody collects something different."

"Is this all you got?" I ask.

He goes on, "There's probably another three thousand up in the attic, ones that were sent to me from all over the country. People on vacation stop in during the summertime, and all of a sudden here comes a package in the mail or UPS with more dolls."

~~~~

There is an old creamery across the street from the park with the gravestones lined up at the back. Out in front are three life-size sculptures. The first, sitting on a brick pier next to the front door, is of a farmer wearing gloves, a seed cap, blue plaid shirt, a pair of jeans, no belt, and sneakers with Velcro straps instead of laces. He is smiling, an arm raised in welcome. In the middle of the neatly groomed yard is a kind of troll made of some unidentifiable brown composite. Unlike the fellow at the door, the troll and his clothes were all fashioned from the same material. He wears a broad though mostly toothless smile and bib overalls with red suspenders; with blue-painted fingernails he holds one hand up in welcome and in the other a metal pole with a wooden plaque that reads, "Ufda." Across his ample belly is a sash that reads, "Belly by Budweiser." And there is more: at the far end of the creamery stands a Viking made of the same material as the troll, wearing a horned helmet on his head and a brown tunic, bearing a blue shield in one hand and a raised sword in the other.

Soon enough, I step inside and, after a little searching and calling out, find a tall, old man in bib overalls and seed cap. He is leaning over the largest lathe I have ever seen, turning what looks like a porch post for an old house. I introduce myself.

"Excuse me. Sorry to just walk in like this, but I had to meet the person who made the sculptures outside."

Without missing a beat, as if it is the most natural thing in the world to have some stranger walk into his workplace asking questions, he introduces himself as Owen Vaaler. Without a pause, in that deep-voiced, Norwegian accent I associate with the old people I grew up around in Albert Lea, he quickly goes about explaining what he is doing.

"I got a call the other day from this man who wanted to replace some porch posts that had rotted away." Pointing to the post in front of him, he says, "This is the only one left that was any good. So I take that post and set it in the lathe like this. Then I put my stock on top of that, and I cut it.

"I don't know if you're familiar with how a lathe works, but"—he explains that the lathe spins—"You see that point there? After I cut it down enough, I just follow along with the point."

I begin to understand, realizing that he uses it as a guide for cutting the new post.

He continues, "And that guides and that duplicates. Like I said, I turn those things out. Well, the first one took me a long time because of setting it up. But the next one, I cut it down in about half an hour. Once I've got the pattern set in there, I can duplicate as many posts as I want."

I am more interested in his sculptures and in particular the trolls. I had spotted a few more in his office when I first walked into the building. But before asking him about that, I ask how he ended up working in an old creamery.

"My dad bought it in the mid-sixties sometime from the Land O'Lakes dairy cooperative. I don't recollect exactly the day, but he bought it. It had stood empty for a few years. He was in the feed business and so converted the building to that purpose. And when he retired, I ran the feed business for a few years and then switched over to fiberglass."

He tells me he had lived on the family farm for many years before taking over at the creamery. "Yeah, I lived about a mile out of town. It's where I was born and lived until I was about eleven years old, and then my dad bought a farm farther out in the country. That's the one that I took over from him. He left the farm and got into the feed business when I got married.

"I had the farm for about fifteen, well, actually, twenty-five years before taking over here. And now my son owns this building. He's the third generation owning it after my dad purchased it."

"Now, Vaaler is a Norwegian name, isn't it?" I ask.

He replies proudly, "Yaah, it's Norwegian, the double 'a' is 'ah.'"

"I grew up in Albert Lea," I tell him. "It's also predominantly Norwegian, though my street was mostly Danish. We moved to Albert Lea from central Illinois in 1963 when I was a little boy. We're German and Irish, which is a pretty typical mix in that part of Illinois. And we came up here, and it's like, 'My god, who are these people?' All of us kids are Catholic because my mom is Catholic, but my dad is Presbyterian, and everybody in Albert Lea is Lutheran."

Following my train of thought, he replies, "You know I've got a pronounced Norwegian accent, but I can't talk Norwegian. I never learned. It's fading out now. There aren't that many people that talk Norwegian as much as they used to, but I have a few classmates that speak it still. So they talk Norwegian to me, and I stand there with a dumb look on my face, and they finally realize that I don't understand what they're talking about."

"Did your folks speak Norwegian at home?"

"My mother was a schoolteacher. She moved here from where she was raised in a German community in Port Washington, Wisconsin. But she was Norwegian. Every year, the first thing she did was to teach the kids how to speak English before she could teach them anything else. So she decided she wasn't going to have that problem with us. So they never talked Norwegian to us, though they both were fluent in it.

"But some people here in town are trying to hang on to it. I mean, there's the Sons of Norway Lodge down here, and that's quite active. There are a lot of members. I suppose the people in the Sons of Norway Lodge now, their average age would be in the mid- to late fifties, probably sixties. That's an average. You go another generation, there may still be a

Sons of Norway Lodge, but there won't be anybody talking Norwegian. In fact, there's very little Norwegian spoken at the lodge now. I belonged to it for a couple of years, but I'm not much of a joiner. Everything is done in English."

We walk over to his office, and I ask, "how did you start making sculptures of trolls?"

"Well, I started out as a kid. Back during the Depression, you couldn't buy a lot of toys, so I made my own. I started doing that, and ever since then, I've made things all my life. When I farmed, I made almost all the stuff I needed to farm with. I always had a project I was making. And then we got into town, and I took over my dad's feed business. I processed my own special brand of feed, and I made all of the equipment to mix the feed and bag it. One of my first projects after I started the fiberglass business was a big feed bin. Then I got into calf hutches. I designed all my own calf hutches. I made all the molds to make them. Basically, I've been making something all my life."

"What's this one all about," I say, pointing to a figure of a bearded man with large ears wearing a pointed cap and green overalls and holding in his right hand what looks like an eagle-headed staff with a snake wrapped around the shaft and in the other a stoneware jug with a corncob stuck in the top.

He says, "It's called *The Healer*. It scares the evil spirits out of you with the hawk and the snake and puts the good spirits back."

I ask, "Did the idea come from a Norwegian folktale?"

He replies, as if addressing a child, "Well, it's a troll."

Why so obvious? I've never seen a troll like this in any collection of Scandinavian folktales I've read. Egging him on, I ask, "He's a troll?"

"Yeah, that's all. I made more of them, too. I've sold quite a few pieces."

A second troll stands on top of a shelf high up the wall. He has a scruffy head of hair beneath a cap and wears an equally scruffy beard on his chin beneath a nose reddened as if he has been drinking. In his left hand he holds a bouquet of pink roses, and in the other a leash at the end of which is attached a skunk.

I ask Owen Vaaler why he made sculptures of trolls, and he tells me they come to him in dreams. Sometimes they tell him their names, and other times he just wakes up to them. He has long, Norwegian-sounding names for them that remind me of Rumpelstiltskin.

How unexpected to find a dreamer of trolls in this small, rural town. But he is, after all, a farmer and a maker of machinery. He cultivates seeds into commodities using the earth, the sun, and rain and imagines machines that extend the reach of a man or woman and then makes them.

Here we are on the edge of the Mississippi River valley and the beginning of the Great Plains: neither one nor the other but becoming simultaneously. Maybe by some magic, something of the old world has survived in this small town, the first Norwegian settlement in the state, something that feels at home in the language, that knows the long nights of winter, the exuberance of spring, the everlasting sunshine of summer—something that conjures up spirits in old men who can scare the evil out of you with a hawk and a snake and revive the good that has always been there.

We talk a little longer, and then I say goodbye and walk back outside into the late-afternoon sun. In the park across the street, the leaves of a maple are turning red. It reminds me of a maple in Lincoln Park near our house in Albert Lea. Early each September it begins to change color, inspiring my mother to say how beautiful and unexpected it is to see all that color with so much green still around.

Riceford, Minnesota

Wending through a grove of hardwoods, the road suddenly descends into the steep-sided valley of Riceford Creek and the little town of Riceford situated along its banks. Most of the town is nestled into the west side of the valley, above which stands the tall spire of an old Lutheran church.

The windows of the church have gone all wavy with age. The pale light of the overcast sky occupies the austere interior, illuminating more than a century of sacramental life and prayer.

Nearby lies a graveyard filled with monuments marking the lives of parishioners who appear to be mostly Norwegian settlers and their descendants. One stone in particular stands out. It marks the untimely deaths of the sons of John and Ingeborg Butler. Arnold Millard died at one week in 1896, and Bennett Peander at a little over two years in 1897. The gravestone takes the form of an unfurled scroll extending down the length of a stack of limestone blocks. A single lily lies on the top, while at the bottom of the scroll a second lily rests among fern fronds. Standing to the side, perched on one of the limestone blocks, a small barefoot boy wearing nothing but a nightshirt leans in toward the scroll, pointing the index finger of his right hand at the names carved into its surface. He has the sweetest face, delicate little ears, eyes, nose, fingers, and toes. Though it has been more than a hundred years since these young boys died, their gravestone still evokes the deep sadness and anguish their parents clearly felt at their passing. How their mother must have wept at the thought of their precious little bodies lying alone in the dark of the cold, hard ground.

At the top of the rise, a second graveyard unexpectedly appears to the left of the road. The gate says that it is the "Old English Cemetery Riceford Minnesota." I cannot resist, so walk through the gate and find myself standing among a couple dozen whitewashed marble stones in tall green grass. Who knows why someone painted the stones. Funny things seem to happen to gravestones in this part of the state.

Most of the names are English. One in particular, Wait, I remember seeing in a graveyard back in Illinois. *Are they related?*

Here in the little town of Riceford, Minnesota, come together two competing narratives of westward expansion. One, the story of the rugged pioneers opening up what they thought had always been a wilderness as they push ever farther into the interior of the continent spreading Western civilization wherever they go. And a second, less often told in history books, of European immigrants fanning out to homestead the land from outposts of settlement founded by the English. They brought with them the languages, folklore, and histories of continental European cultures that all in time have been subsumed by the dominant narrative of the English-speaking history of America.

What must these first English-speaking settlers have thought, seeing the land they had settled turned over to a strange people, speaking a foreign language and following an austere faith? Just as they had displaced the first Americans, now Scandinavian immigrants in turn were replacing them. The number of monuments in the graveyard at the Lutheran church continues to grow, while this cemetery has not seen a new burial since before the turn of the twentieth century. Where had the English gone? Moved off, died out, or married into local Scandinavian families to become nothing more than a genealogical footnote.

Yet a third narrative underlies them both. The wilderness was of our own making. Millions of native peoples lived here before us. They cultivated a land and created a civilization. First it was disease, then murder, then removal. Some of us committed these atrocities others benefited from them. We may only see shadows, but they still live in broad daylight. We wake up to the same sun and all sleep beneath the same stars.

Platt Deutsch

I have walked about thirty miles since crossing the Minnesota border. With Harmony not far ahead, I see a group of farmsteads without electrical service. There are no transformers hanging from the poles carrying the electrical lines alongside the road or secondary lines leading to the farmsteads. It is an Amish community. Unlike historic sites from the nineteenth century, these homes and outbuildings are not restored museum pieces, exercises in preserving the past. They are real-time homes and workplaces for people who, though they practice a nineteenth-century way of life, are very much alive in the twenty-first.

They lack the uniformly even gravel drives and concrete-floored machine sheds of modern farms. The farmhouses bear the marks that only large families with muddy feet leave behind. And unlike the homes of the "English," whose closed windows and enclosed porches suggest an air-conditioned inwardness, these homes have open windows and broad, wraparound porches designed to catch the slightest breeze. Yet on this day the porches are empty and the windows look out blankly on the world.

Shortly thereafter, a young Amish man comes up from the opposite direction. Though he sees me, he walks with his head down, his long brown beard sticking out from under his broad-brimmed straw hat.

I call out, "Guten Tag! Heute ist ein schones Tag, Ja? Wie gehts du?"

He does not say anything, so I call out once more, "Guten Tag!"

As he walks by, he responds. As he looks up from beneath his cap, I see brown eyes and a large, flat, suntanned face. Speaking in a curious mix of country and German accents, he tells me in English that the Amish do not speak Hoch Deutsch, but instead speak Platt Deutsch. And that is that.

Harmony, Minnesota

Looking like someone's grandmother, an elderly woman stands behind the front desk at the Country Lodge Inn in Harmony, Minnesota. On the wall behind her is a print of a blond Jesus surrounded by "It's a Small World," doe-eyed children, a portrait of John Wayne as Rooster Cogburn from *True Grit*, Elvis in black velvet (of course), and several photographs of President G. W. Bush, some with the old woman and who must be her husband standing alongside.

Harmony is a nice little farm town of about a thousand people that has done well in recent years from the Amish tourist trade as well as from people visiting the hill country of southeastern Minnesota, nearby Niagara Cave, Forestville State Park, and the Harmony-Preston Valley bicycle trail. Downtown is noteworthy more for its antique shops and stores selling Amish handicrafts than for services for local residents.

It is 7:00 PM on a Sunday, so I am worried there might not be anywhere to eat. But the Harmony House Inn is open and surprisingly busy. Everyone inside seems local. Most of the tourists have probably already returned to the Twin Cities. Given the extent of the tourist trade here, the residents must be used to strangers. I am just part of the general annoyance suffered by towns with no choice other than to manufacture quaintness if they are going to survive. If anyone does take notice, it will be because it is a Sunday night and I should already have gone back to where I came from.

The waitress is talking to some people in a booth when she sees me. She walks over and says, "The kitchen closes in five minutes, so if you want anything you better sit down where you can find an empty seat, and I'll be over to you when

I'm finished here." She grabs a menu off a nearby table, hands it to me, then walks off to another and puts down their bill.

There is a booth at the back. The waitress arrives soon enough with a knife, fork, spoon, paper napkin, and placemat, and takes my order. "I'll have a bacon cheeseburger with fries and a side of coleslaw, please."

Though the restaurant has begun to clear out, there are still plenty of people finishing their meals. A booth nearby is filled with disheveled children and a couple of exhausted parents. There is a table with two elderly couples drinking coffee. A middle-aged guy with a scraggly blond beard wearing a dirty T-shirt that rides high up on his ample belly sits alone at the counter, looking ahead at nothing in particular. The manager in shirtsleeves stands behind the register near the door, talking to someone on the phone while ringing up some others who are finished and on their way.

It must have been a diner for many years, but those years were of steadily declining revenues. Though it makes enough to stay open, likely cycling through owners thinking they have the recipe for success, it never earns enough to cover the costs of maintenance and upkeep. The fixtures are worn out or replaced with increasingly less expensive alternatives so the place looks like it has been decorated out of a cold and musty discount restaurant supply outlet. Bare fluorescent tubes in fixtures screwed directly into a yellowed drywall ceiling make everyone inside look a little nauseous.

I sit there thinking about all the conversations going on around me. I have become unused to talking to people. You can ask someone for directions, something of the history of their town, or even why they live the way they do and remain aloof and inward looking. I am content to eat my dinner alone. Talking to someone seems beyond my reach at this moment. I eat in silence and leave as soon as I am finished.

~~~~

As I walk to the motel,
The night gathers around me.
The last fragments of birdsong fade into the twilight.
Porch lights flicker in the shifting leaves like twinkling stars
As constellations sweep across the night sky
Beyond the haze of brightening street lamps.

Forestville State Park

Forestville is a ghost town. Founded in the 1850s, it was bypassed by the railroad and, like many towns in similar circumstances, faded away as families left for more prosperous locales. In the end, all that remained was a general store owned by the Meighen family, one of the town's founders, and that too closed at the turn of the last century. And there it stood undisturbed for sixty years, when the state took possession of the building and discovered that the contents of the store were still in place. A member of the Meighen family closed a door and turned a key, locking in a moment in time.

I visited the park when I was a teenager, and I soon discover that things have changed since my brief stay all those years ago. What had been a newly opened historic site, still a bit dusty and untouched by curators of living history, is now occupied by local antiquarians and the odd teenager historically reenacting the 1890s. I liked it better when I had to guess the use of an unfamiliar wooden tool rather than being embarrassed by the eager demonstrations of someone with an unhealthy attachment to the past—like the person who has played the wench or village idiot just a few summers too many at the local renaissance fair.

My campsite is near the south fork of the Root River. I sit at the picnic table as the twilight gathers up the silence around me. After a summer overrun by families in tents and pop-ups, there is very little grass left and the whole place smells faintly of grilled hamburgers, hot dogs, and spilled pop.

Feeling their presence, I am conscious of every sound I make. Haunted by their absence, I quickly eat my dinner, clean up, and put away my kit. I sit down again in silence.

So many lives that meant so much to the living are now forgotten, as if they were never there. The past means nothing to the dead. These people I see in graveyards, no one knows they ever existed. Seventy, eighty years on the face of this earth, and then they're gone. Done. Dead, buried, and gone. If there is life after death, it is not lived here.

Done. I ache for it sometimes. Done and gone. Past, present, and future—all gone. Yet, despite everything he did to imprison my soul, I am still here. Part of me is still free.

I get up and walk over to the river. At this point it is little more than a stream. I sit down on the bank and watch its shifting currents. The light is far enough off the midpoint of the day that I can see small brown trout hovering over the sandy bottom. Not long thereafter I realize that I am not alone. About ten yards upstream, perched on a broken limb extended over the edge of the water, sits a kingfisher poised intently in search of the same trout I am looking at. We sit there together for a while. When I stand up it flies from its perch into the shadows already gathering in the trees above.

~~~~

Across a landscape of green dissolving into blue,

I walk west toward the unobstructed line

Of an ever-receding horizon.

Mile after mile of sameness . . .

Following a yellow road through hissing fields

My mind wanders from the sky

To my uninterrupted footsteps.

The living rhythm of my body.

Alone in a Strange House

Thirty-six miles east of Albert Lea, I arrive in Adams, Minnesota. Like so many other small towns, downtown Adams has fallen on hard times. Yet it still has a high school, a cooperative grain elevator, and a new wind farm whose enormous turbines tower over the south side of town.

Across the street from Bubble's Café, whose name does more to recommend it than its worn-out exterior, stands one of my favorite buildings in the area: the old First National State Bank of Adams, designed by the Minneapolis firm of Purcell & Elmslie, a sweet little example of Prairie School architecture completely unlike anything else in town. It is a small, rectangular structure constructed of red brick with a large, rectangular, west-facing window framed in terracotta. Though much of its original ornament has been shorn away, I am happy to see it still standing.

Built in a progressive era, it symbolized the community's dreams of a prosperous future. Neither the dream nor the building has emerged unscathed by recent decades of neglect and disinvestment. Empty now, it most recently was a liquor store.

I hope to camp out near the Church of the Sacred Heart, but I cannot find anyone to ask. The doors are locked at the church and elementary school. And though both the front and side doors of the priest's house are open, no one answers my repeated knocking. Too tired to be discouraged, I walk back to the café to eat and gather some local intelligence on alternatives for the night.

Everything at Bubble's Café is made from scratch. The food is first-rate. Before long, I start talking to Janet, the owner. I tell her about my rotten luck at the Catholic church. With no motel in town, I fear I am out of luck. She suggests I call a local attorney.

She tells me, "He's a nice young man and a good Christian. He'll be here shortly. He's coming by to pick up a tray of cookies on his way down to Iowa for a youth fellowship meeting in Stacyville."

Before too long, in walks a nice-looking guy, about average height with dark brown hair, who must be my age or a little younger. Janet introduces us. I tell him I am walking home to Albert Lea from Chicago and looking for a place to spend the night. He looks me over and says he is happy to put me up for the night. He tells me, "I've got an extra bedroom, so there's plenty of room."

He grabs a tray of cookies, and I grab my pack, thank Janet for her help, and follow him out the door. There are two other guys in the car, so after some rearranging we make the short trip to the north side of town, where he drops me off at his house.

They are in a hurry. "I don't have time to show you around. We're already running late. Just make yourself at home. Oh, and don't stay up for me because we won't be back until late. Maybe I'll see you in the morning?"

And with that they are off, leaving me standing alone in the driveway. I am dying for a cookie, but he did not offer, and I did not ask.

The house is a split-level ranch with an attached two-car garage. Inside, I find the spare bedroom up a short flight of stairs. The bed is made, and the room is clean. There are no pictures on the walls. It is not until I walk around the rest of the house that things get a little strange.

The kitchen sink is full of dirty dishes, and the counters are cluttered with mail and miscellaneous stuff that appears to have been hanging around longer than it should. The furniture in the living room is in that unfortunate seventies' dorm lounge, American Indestructible style, with two-by-four wooden arms and frames and large upholstered foam seats and backs done in a crazy Scottish plaid. The furniture looks knocked about by someone who has not bothered to put it back in place.

What lamps there are have shades askew and ripped. The walls are all white and empty except for a couple framed prints hanging this way and that. The print media left lying around is all Christian: Christian pamphlets and tracts, Christian magazines and tabloids, Christian everything.

There is an entertainment center with a television, VCR, and CD player. All the videotapes and CDs are Christian. There is not a single non-Christian piece of literature in the whole house. With some anxiety, I walk back up the steps and into his bedroom.

Like the spare bedroom, it is sparsely decorated but clean. He has a king-size bed and a wide dresser with a large mirror done in the same style as the living-room furniture. Sitting on the dresser is a series of framed photographs documenting the progress of a relationship: there he is alongside a young woman with blonde hair and an attractive smile at dinner in a restaurant, with friends during a backyard cookout, at a Twins game up in the Cities, on what looks like the deck of a cruise ship, on the streets of some coastal Mexican tourist town, at their wedding shower surrounded by gift wrap and admiring friends, and, finally, holding hands with family flanked on either side at their wedding. I see myself in the mirror standing alone in a bedroom that shows no sign of any occupant other than my absent host.

Looking closer, I see return-address labels stuck in the mirror's frame. Each reads, "Mr. and Mrs. Hatcher." One after another, lining the entire edge of the mirror from top to bottom and side to side.

Back in the spare bedroom with the door shut, I lie down on the bed. It is disturbing to spend the night surrounded by such sadness. The painful longing for intimacy can be terrible. Though Jesus is present everywhere, I suspect He provides little consolation in those dark moments before sleep in an empty house made unbearable by the absence of the woman this man loves.

The morning arrives dark and cold. I get up, dress, and pull on my pack, which I had gotten ready the night before. When I step out of the room, he is sitting up in his bed, awake.

With a pleasant smile, he asks, "How was your night?"

"Good. Thanks for letting me stay. I really appreciate it," I reply.

He says, "God bless and good luck on the road." And then after a moment, "Jesus was a pilgrim, too, you know."

"Thank you." And I am out the door.

The street lamps go out and dawn arrives. A thermometer above a storefront reads forty-six degrees. It is September in Minnesota. I stop to put on my thermo vest, zipping it up over my shirt.

Broken Glass

Our brokenness is in our hearts.
It is the starting point of our humanity.

Bohemian National Cemetery

Late in the afternoon, the tall pine and cedar trees encircling the old Bohemian Cemetery on the east side of Freeborn County emerge from the fields.

A car approaches and slows down. I am getting a little unsteady on my feet, having walked twenty-five miles since leaving Adams. I am not thinking clearly. The car crosses over the centerline and steers toward me. I am about to jump down into the ditch when I see that it is my mom and dad. I thought that big beige Mercury looked familiar.

I called the night before to tell them I would spend the night camped out at the cemetery then walk the last thirteen miles into town in the morning. They clearly had other ideas.

They pull up, and my mom gets out of the passenger side, laughing. "I can't believe it! You made it! You walked all the way from Chicago just to come home! I can't believe it!"

My dad waits in the car while my mom hugs me.

Telling more than asking, my mom says, "Why don't you get in the car and we'll drive you over to the cemetery and sit down in the shade?" I hesitate a little. Then I get in the car.

Soon enough we pull into the graveyard, get out, sit down in the shade, and talk. My parents sit on a concrete bench while I lie down on the grass and take off my shoes and socks. Sitting there looking into my mother's sparkling eyes and listening to her laughing voice, for the first time in a long time I feel what must be the love that grew inside me as a baby in her arms. Perhaps this long, quiet walk from the state where I was born to where I grew up has reawakened in me the unencumbered love a small child has for his mother.

My father asks, "Why don't you let us drive you home?"

I reply, "On one condition: that you drive me back out here tomorrow morning so I can walk into town on my own. I've been telling everyone that I'm walking home, so that's what I'm going to do."

We laugh at my determination. They are both in their mid-seventies. My mother's name is Rita and my dad Dick. She has a round face and red cheeks. She wears her hair in a permanent and speaks in a musical voice. My dad has a gray come-over, is stocky, and has sallow skin. My mom teases him about it. "Dick, you always look sick."

My mother sings in a church choir at funerals. She calls them "The Dead Beats." Some funerals are very sad with only one mourner or none. Everyone else in his or her life is gone. Others are terrible. The church is full of people crying over the death of someone too young to die.

My dad loves sports, any kind of sports. He was a star athlete in high school lettering in football, basketball, and track. Among my fondest memories is sitting in the TV room with him watching golf tournaments. I loved how the announcers whispered. My dad is the kind of guy who reaches out his hand to someone and with self-confidence verging on bravado announces that he is "Dick Herwig. Nice to meet you." My mother says, "Your father is a man who knows no strangers." But today he doesn't have much to say. He is happy to let my mom do the talking.

Mom hands me an orange and an over-ripe banana. "I grabbed them off the kitchen table on our way out the door. I couldn't come empty handed."

I hand her back the banana and eat the orange.

We visit a little about how my sister and brothers are doing, the latest from the extended family, life in Albert Lea, and what people are doing to halt its unstoppable decline.

My mom asks if I got the book she sent me a week before I left Chicago. I remind her that I did and thanked her for it. She says, "You know your father and I didn't think this walk was a good idea. It would be too dangerous. We worried you'd get run over and end up dead in a ditch. But you insisted you were going to do it. And we realized there was nothing we could do about it. You're a grown man after all. It was then that we understood that you were in search of something and far be it from us to try and stand in your way.

I was at the Hallmark Store around this time and came across a book called *The Meaning of Life*. We read it to each other that night and knew we had to send it to you. It says how we feel and that we support you and your walk."

The front cover of the book has a photo of a frog looking at you and the back a chimpanzee sitting in a pose like Rodin's *The Thinker*. Each page has a line or two of text along the bottom and a photo of an animal in an anthropomorphic posture reinforcing the message of the text.

The book begins with a baby fur seal with cocked head. Beneath in green ink it reads, "No matter how you look at it, life is strange." The last two pages, with a smiling chimp pointing to his head on the first and a cat leaning one paw over what looks like a fence on the other, reads "You know something else? If you just listen with your heart and use your head, you'll never be wrong."

My mother inscribed the book to me on the inside front cover. "Dear Tim, This expresses how we now feel about your trip 'home.' Read & enjoy. Love you so, Mom and Dad."

Soon enough, we are in the car driving home. I spend the night in the bedroom I shared with my brothers Paul and Tom. I recognize the weight of the door and the click it makes when I close it. The luminescent Guardian Angel switch plate glows with a ghostly light as I lie down in darkness and fall asleep.

Albert Lea Lake Stinks

My dad drives off from the cemetery, and I begin the final stretch on my own. The plan is to meet at the Elks Club for lunch.

It is not long before I reach the eastern shore of Albert Lea Lake, one of the most polluted lakes in the state of Minnesota. Not only has it been the repository of 150 years of soil erosion and more recently chemical fertilizer and pesticide runoff, but it was also where the city's sewage treatment plant, the local meatpacking plant, and a foundry discharged their collective wastewater. Just about everything nasty from Albert Lea and the surrounding watershed makes its way into the lake, and from there down the Shell Rock River to the Cedar, the Iowa, and then the Mississippi, ending up in the waters of the Gulf of Mexico. In the 1970s, people drove around with bumper stickers reading, "Albert Lea Lake Stinks."

It has always been a broad, shallow prairie lake, one of the biggest in southern Minnesota. And before a dam was put in at the mouth of the Shell Rock River, large stretches of it receded into wetland as the year turned to autumn, then after the springtime thaw rose up once again with waves lapping at its shoreline.

Like most living things, it had a rhythm, a rhythm that has been stopped for those boaters brave enough to venture out on its polluted waters. There it sits, bloated and obese, accumulating toxins and dying a long, slow death.

But, on this beautiful late-summer morning, as I look out on its reflective blue waters through the branches of the hardwoods that line its shores, flocks of waterfowl float on the water—Canada geese, mallards, coots, and ringnecks, small groupings of white pelicans readying to migrate south, and the occasional blue heron stalking its prey in the shallows.

~~~~

St. Nicholas Park stands above the lake's southern shore. A pink granite marker, looking every bit the glacial erratic, placed by the Daughters of the American Revolution in the 1920s, marks the spot of the first European settlement in Freeborn County in 1855. The village of St. Nicholas disappeared shortly thereafter. The town's residents moved on to other communities, either taking their homes with them or selling them off to local farmers, who dismantled them and hauled them away to be used as new homes or outbuildings. These were practical people. They did not leave anything behind that could be put to use.

We took long drives around the lake on Sunday afternoons when I was a boy. It was on one of those drives in the mid-sixties that we stopped at the park and first discovered the marker. Even then I remember how odd it was to stand there on the spot of that long-vanished community knowing that neither I nor anyone in my family had any connection to it.

I never really felt at home in Minnesota until I left Albert Lea for college. And though I have come to love the state's climate and geography, its history of progressive labor and populist politics, even its Scandinavian ethnicity, its dour Lutheranism, and the earnest self-righteousness of its liberal politics, I have never shaken off the influence of those early days of otherness in Albert Lea.

Standing here, I remember the family stories we told and realize how they gave voice to an underlying history of love that bound us together. Each family story signified that, though with time and distance we may become strangers to each other, we all came into the world out of the same act of love.

Both my parents grew up in Pontiac, Illinois in the central part of the state. Once, when my dad was playing hide and seek with his sisters and brothers and mother, she hid by squeezing herself between the toilet and the wall. Of course, she got stuck. They had to call a plumber to dismantle the toilet to get her out.

My dad's Uncle Lou and Aunt Ella were fond of his younger brother Jim. One day they walked across the street from where they lived and told my grandparents they were going to adopt Jim. Uncle Lou told my grandparents that they already had plenty of kids and anyway Jim liked them better. That was the last time they spoke to each other. Jim stayed. Who knows how long they tried, but Lou and Ella had never been able to have children.

When my parents were dating in high school, my dad once borrowed his brother-in-law's car and drove over to my mom's house to take her to a movie downtown. He lived on the north side and my mom on the south side. It was during the Second World War so gas was rationed. There was a slight incline from south to north so after picking up my mom, they drove a short distance back north on Mill Street, shut off the engine, and glided the rest of the way to the movie theater.

My mother's father died on New Year's Eve 1944. One of her last memories of her father was his sitting in front of the radio wrapped in a blanket, wracked with cancer, and anxiously listening to news of the War. All of his sons were in the military.

My mother's mother, who we called Nana, stayed with us every year for a couple weeks or a couple months at a time. She slept with my sister Patty in the same bed. If she were with us during the summer, on particularly hot days, she'd sit in the backyard in the shade. She opened her blouse several buttons to cool off. When it came time to eat, my mother would send one of us out to bring her in. We hated doing this as it too often involved seeing her ancient flat breasts as she turned to acknowledge us, not bothering to button up.

Right after Patty was born, my mother flew from Chicago to Tacoma, Washington to meet my father at Fort Lewis where he was stationed during the Korean War. It was an old prop. She held my sister tight and didn't get up once to use the bathroom afraid the plane might tilt over and crash.

My mom once found Patty and my brother Rick sliding down a neighbor's backyard slide naked calling out over and over again "Bare But! Bare But!"

I can remember the smile on my sister Patty's face holding her sixteenth birthday cake. She looked so beautiful.

My brothers Rick and Mark were playing cops and robbers with metal cap guns. Though younger, Mark was always quicker and cleverer than Rick. So once when he had the chance and Mark poked his head around a corner, Rick threw his gun at him, knocking out his front teeth.

My brother Tom ate his peanut butter sandwiches upside down so they wouldn't stick to the roof of his mouth. He ate his food delicately with his fingers, rarely using utensils. When he chewed his jaw clicked. I always sat next to him at the supper table. I spent my entire childhood slightly nauseous whenever we ate.

The youngest, my brother Paul, can't see a foot in front of his face without his glasses. When he was eighteen months old, my parents got him his first pair. He opened his eyes so wide that she was sure he saw the world as it really is for the very first time.

I stand in the park and listen to the wind. It has picked up and is blowing out of the southwest, silencing all other sounds except the wavelike rise and fall of the surrounding vegetation.

The park is overshadowed by a grove of oak trees. Their otherwise gray bark is speckled with blue and yellow lichens. In stark contrast to the movement around them, the trunks of the trees remain arrestingly still. The sunlight broken up by the windblown leaves and branches scatters across the grass like broken glass.

The Elks Club

My parents sit at a table in the semi-gloom of the dining room. The place still has the feel of a smoky, fifties-era supper club. Had I walked through the bar when I entered, the same men would certainly have been sitting there having a drink who were there forty years ago, only now permanently stooped and considerably grayer.

After we moved to Albert Lea, my parents found their first friends at the Elks Club. Their closest friends were Tom and Jean Speltz, Mary and Ray Keating, and Hilmer and Gen Opp. Beginning in the early sixties and carrying on through the nineties, they met on the occasional Saturday evening, ate dinner, and danced late into the night to music performed by local combos like the Rollie Green Trio, Neil and Barbara Lang, and Rollo Sissel, who made the drive over from Austin.

Sitting across from my parents now, I can imagine them gathered around the table with their friends, taking a break from the dance floor, telling stories and laughing, drinking beer and cocktails. A candle burns in a red glass at the center of the table, showing damp breasts through loosely buttoned blouses, strands of hair flat on sweaty foreheads, and mounds of bouffant hair glistening through the dim light and cigarette smoke.

During my sophomore year in high school, my dad helped me get a job at the Elks washing dishes on Friday and Saturday nights. I worked alongside a woman named Elaine. She was tall and very thin, had short salt-and-pepper hair, and always wore light-blue polyester uniforms with a white apron wrapped around her waist. With a series of cigarettes held firmly between her red lips, lips whose color gradually faded and became patchy over the course of the night, she worked silently next to me, rarely looking up from the stainless steel tubs before us. We washed all the dishes and pans by hand.

The only person she ever exchanged words with was the head cook, Anita Borland. Anita was a force of nature, and in running the kitchen felt she had rights to run the whole club. Though I thought she was terrific, she was not much liked by the membership. She was given to walking out into the dining room, her big hands pushing back hair matted with sweat, wearing a much-stained apron around her ample waist, and expressing her opinions on management to anyone who was unlucky enough to listen.

My first night on the job, she asked what I wanted to eat after the last customer was served. I had never had a filet mignon, so I politely asked for that. When I told her I wanted it well done, she stopped what she was doing and informed me that I was getting it rare or not at all. I quickly acquiesced. Shortly thereafter, with the entire kitchen staff sitting around a table, she served me up my bloody filet with a spiced red apple as a garnish and a side of hash browns. When I asked for ketchup, she nearly got up from the table in disgust. "No, you are not having ketchup. You're not going to ruin my steak with ketchup. You'd think Dick and Rita would have raised you to know at least that!" She went on until, pulling a dirty hand towel from out of her belt, she wiped her brow and calmed down enough to eat her own meal.

Aside from the occasional terse exchange with Anita, Elaine otherwise only talked to broken or chipped water glasses. The Elks water glasses were heavy, red tumblers.

It went something like this, "Oh, you poor pretty thing. Now that you're broken, no one will ever want you anymore. Well, I'll take care of you. I'll clean you up and take you home with me."

And then she'd wash it, speaking to it in mumbling whimpers as if it were a child. "Oh, honey, now you're nice and clean, all shiny and red. Sit there where I can keep an eye on you, and tonight, when I'm through here, I'll take you home like I promised."

One sunny Saturday afternoon before I went to work, I rode my bicycle around town and happened down the street where Elaine and her brother Jerry lived. Jerry was a little older and taller, though just as thin as Elaine. He wore his gray hair long, down to his shoulders. We often saw him walking around town at a quick clip, always more than a little drunk. He did not seem to work.

As I rode down the street wondering which among the worn-out houses was theirs, I saw Jerry wander into a particularly beat-up one. Not really thinking about what I was doing, I rode up their driveway, parked my bike, and walked up to the door and knocked. No answer. I tried the door. It was unlocked. I walked in.

I walked down a dark hallway into the living room. It smelled of damp, musty carpets and furniture. Once my eyes grew accustomed to the dim light, I noticed that both Elaine and her brother were watching television with the volume turned off while listening to an old Frank Sinatra record.

Jerry sat on the couch next to Elaine, who was smoking. They looked up at me as I walked in.

"Hi," I said. "I was just riding by on my bike and saw Jerry walk in. And I thought, hey, that must be where Elaine lives. So I thought I should drop by and say hello before work tonight. You know, we have to work tonight? So I parked my bike out front and walked up to the door and knocked. No one answered, so knowing that someone was home, I just walked in. Hi!"

Jerry shifted uncomfortably in his seat; Elaine took a drag off her cigarette and turned back to the television. They did not say a word.

I noticed that the walls were covered in an old floral-print wallpaper and the shades were all pulled down and the curtains drawn so only a hint of bright sunshine leaked in.

The longer I stood there, the more I noticed the place smelled. Now very self-conscious, I said, "Well, I guess I should be going. It was nice to meet you, Jerry. See you tonight, Elaine. Bye."

I quickly left. Once outside and on my bicycle, I looked back and noticed that all the interior windowsills were lined with broken and chipped glasses blazing red in the sunlight.

The Long Way Home

My dad managed the local Spurgeon's Department Store downtown, and my mom worked at the Credit Bureau. She usually got home from work shortly after three, to be there when we got back from school. Then at around five-thirty, those of us who were home piled into the car, and she drove downtown to pick up my dad from work. She parked out front, and we clambered out of the car, raced through the front door, and immediately dropped to our hands and knees, the younger ones giggling and the older ones shushing, and crawled directly toward the glass and stainless-steel candy cases. Once behind them, we reached up, slid open the doors at the back, and grabbed as much candy as we could hold in our small hands.

At this point, my dad, who had watched the whole thing from up in his office at the back of the store, let out a yell, and we scattered, our fingers wet with melted chocolate, sticky with hard candy, or tacky from multicolored gumdrops. Later on, after he had gotten us all out of the store, he dropped a buck or two into the till to cover the damage, then locked up, giving the front door a firm shake before turning toward the car and the ride home.

We drove north on Broadway and then took a right down Clark Street, where it swung north again onto Bridge Street at the base of the hill. Following the eastern shore of the lake, we crossed over the dam and drove until we reached the light at Johnson Street. There we took a left past the flying red Pegasus of the Mobile gas station, until we reached Valley, where we ordinarily went to the right and soon thereafter arrived home.

But more often than not, I let out a cry of protest, "Go straight, Dad! Let's take the long way home!" Taking the long way home meant continuing on Johnson up a hill, then down again and along the northeast shore of Fountain Lake, past the beach, alongside Pioneer Park, and past the old cemetery.

Though not wanting to return to a small, overcrowded, and chaotic house may have had something to do with my plea, I believe it had more to do with my wishing I were out under a summer sun swimming at the beach, or watching the last glimmer of fall color fade from the trees lining the shore at sunset, or watching the snow blow off the frozen surface of the lake, across the road, and through our passing headlights, or simply taking in the smell of wetness in springtime for just a little longer, surprised yet again by the windswept motion of the water after so many months of icy stillness.

No Longer There . . .

Like many people who grew up in big families with busy parents, I was a lonely boy and teenager. My older brothers were angry and resentful that they did not get enough attention from our parents. They argued with my mother and fought with my dad. They were rough with my younger brother and me and intimidated my sister, who was the oldest. She did what she could to protect herself. Desperate for love and attention, she allied with our mother, spying on my older brothers. It only made matters worse for her. My parents were too busy keeping us clothed and fed to notice any of this. It was only a daughter's closeness to her mother and boyish roughhousing as far as they were concerned. The rest of us hung on tenterhooks, in fear of what might happen next.

The love that brought us into the world was never enough to protect us from our own anger, hurt, and frustration. I learned how to disappear at home and look outside my family for love and intimacy. The problem was that I did not know what those things were. Into this ignorance stepped Robert Williamson.

Remembering

I walk slowly through town on my way to the old high school. The main entrance is blocked by a chain-link fence. It will soon be a parking lot. I sit down beneath its carved stone lintel and remember how it began on a November morning in my junior year.

~~~~

The day had started with a phone call and the news that my grandfather had died. He was my dad's father and the only grandfather I knew. He was eighty-four and had lived with my grandmother in Pontiac, Illinois.

We spent two weeks at their house each summer when I was growing up. My fondest memories are of taking walks with my grandfather uptown when he needed to get out of the house. I remember the excitement I felt walking along with him, working hard to keep up with his long stride, my small hand held in his. Unlike my grandmother, who smothered us with kisses and held us in breathless embraces as tightly to her ample bosom as our little bodies could bear, my grandfather rarely touched us.

Once uptown, my grandfather talked to old men I did not know but who had known my family for years. Old men with tired faces and alert eyes, wearing summer short-sleeved shirts, slacks, and straw hats, who called my grandfather "Whitey" and asked who I belonged to. "Oh, he's one of Dick's boys. They're all staying with us. They drove down from Minnesota." They sometimes talked about my dad's high school athletic achievements, or how I looked like him, or perhaps more like my mother, whom they knew as one of those Jobst girls.

In their eyes I saw a history that I only experienced in Pontiac. They looked into mine and remembered childhoods lived before the wars, before the Depression, before the twentieth century. In my face they remembered the faces of the boys and men, now dead, who came before me.

Most of these conversations ended with the sharp pain of an old man's pinch on the ear like a priest's admonition that we are dust and to dust we shall return. Others rested a warm hand on my head or cupped my cheek and in my eyes saw a boy at the beginning of life looking back at an old man near its end.

My grandfather had a heart attack while replacing damaged shingles on the roof of the house. He climbed down the ladder, walked into the living room, and lay down on the couch. He called out to my grandmother, "Addie, I think it's time." He was rushed to the hospital, where he died the next day.

I took the news hard, though I did not realize how hard until I got to school. It was in Paul Goodnature's first-period junior humanities class. His classroom was just down from Robert Williamson's, where the desk was situated so he could look out into the hallway.

Sitting in Paul's classroom, as the initial shock faded I felt the weight of my loss. The past fell away, and I was no longer able to ignore the uncertainty of the present. Crushed; my lungs fail. I run from the classroom and down the hall. Panic! Suffocating panic! Violent, chest-heaving convulsions!

"I can't breathe!"

Eyes closed, I surrender to the convulsions—waiting for calm to return. Fearful that the convulsions will return, I take a breath, first shallow, then more deeply, and again.

I knew what to do, as I had hyperventilated most of my childhood when roughed up by my older brothers. As it turned out, this episode would be the last.

I didn't know it at the time, but Mr. Williamson had witnessed everything. What did he see that morning in the hallway outside his classroom door? A teenage boy who lost his breath? But why? Most certainly he witnessed the depth of my emotional distress and vulnerability. He saw a young person to occupy. He saw a teenager to entrap with the promise of self-knowledge, and then seduce, feeding off a fear of vulnerability and rejection. Like a shark scenting blood in the ocean, the hunt was on.

After that, he took an active interest in me. It was not long before I was spending increasingly more time at his house, talking about history, literature, and psychology and listening to music. I got to know his wife, adult daughter, and granddaughter. I babysat for his granddaughter, but it was always at Robert's house.

He seduced me, though I pretended it wasn't happening. Indifferent to myself, ignorant of the consequences, and with nothing left to let go, I let him in.

Over the course of my junior year, my sense of self outpaced and outgrew the development of my body. I spilled out of my body to inform and be informed by the world around me. No longer clear where I ended and the world began, everything around me became an extension of myself. The world was simultaneously my most intimate self and a most inscrutable mystery. And into this adolescent landscape Robert Williamson pursued me.

By summer of my junior year, he had planned a trip to the Boundary Waters Canoe Area. He initially told me he planned on bringing along other students. My parents were fine with this plan. But by the time he told me I would be the only one, they were unwilling to take on my disappointment and anger had they refused to let me go.

We left on a Saturday morning early in June and headed north in his golden Dodge sedan, an aluminum Grumman canoe attached to the roof and Robert at the wheel, chain-smoking and talking to me.

At last we drove around a curve and down the steep slope into the city of Duluth. From there we continued up the North Shore of Lake Superior. Towns fell away and the shoreline became more and more rugged. The air was sweet and invigorating, with the smell of pine and fresh water. The landscape was rocky and rugged, cut through by deep ravines down which fast-flowing rivers fell on their way to the lake. The sky took on a different hue, and the clouds that passed before it gathered in unfamiliar configurations.

The landscape was scarred and scraped raw by the receding glaciers, lakes gouged out of boulders and rock, bluffs of granite where mountains once stood, covered by birch and poplar, spruce and cedar, where white pine once towered, and at its heart Lake Superior, an upwelling of geologic time, a well of memory so enormous, so deep and cold that it resisted understanding.

I felt that I had discovered the landscape into which I would pass into adulthood: the beginning of life's adventure. Riding alongside my Gandalf, I was Frodo, on a quest not to destroy a source of great evil but in discovery of myself, the brilliant jewel of self-knowledge at the root of the new life outstretched before me.

We arrived in Grand Marais and spent the night at the Shoreline Inn, a 1950s-era motel stretched out along the shore of the lake. We slept in the same room in separate beds.

When we were alone in the motel room, I pretended I could deflect his desire, but in public, it was impossible. What were others thinking? *Was I his son? Was I his nephew? What was this high school kid doing with a man so clearly not related, yet old enough to be his father?*

We drove up the Gunflint Trail the next morning to our access point on Bearskin Lake. The trail had originally been a logging road into the lake country north along the Canadian border. By the mid-1970s it was largely used to access the BWCA and the region's lodges and resorts. Soon enough, we were in the canoe paddling down the lake. We were on our way to Rose Lake, on the Canadian border. There we camped and spent the better part of a week paddling the nearby lakes.

I took off my shirt one hot afternoon while we were out in the canoe. He insisted on applying sunscreen to my back. As he rubbed in the lotion, he complimented me on how the muscles in my back and upper arms had already developed over the past few days.

I was falling in love with the wilderness, the invigorating freshness of the air, the rocky terrain, the impossible clarity and depth of the waters. I felt like I was being initiated into a society of outdoorsmen who valued the wilderness for its power to instill spiritual renewal through physical beauty and rigorous exercise. Robert spoke a great deal about Sigurd Olson and the story of establishing the BWCA. He recited from memory a quotation from *The Singing Wilderness.* "Wilderness to the people of America is a spiritual necessity, an antidote to the pressure of modern life, a means of regaining serenity and equilibrium."

But of course, it was all a pretext to seduce me. He took me there to imprint the fiction that he was the instrument of my self-awareness. Taking me out of time and place, he drew me into a wilderness of lies, stripped me of my newly developing sense of personal power, and supplanted in its place a dependency so pervasive that my thoughts and feelings were no longer my own. They were his.

June nights in the north country are cool, so each evening I lie near the fire, mesmerized by the flames and absentmindedly stirring the coals with a stick. And then when I was sufficiently warm, I stepped away from the light of the fire through the cool night air down to the lake. The dark still waters mirrored the sky bright with stars.

Evenings around the campfire began with what had already become characteristic of our relationship. Robert, using what he described as the Socratic method, began interrogating me. He convinced me that my uncertainties and loneliness were really a lack of self-esteem. He offered to be my friend. He offered to help me become a feeling person, a "feeling realist," as he called it.

"Who are you, Tim?" he asked. And I replied, "I don't know." And then he repeated, "Who are you, Tim?" And again I replied that I didn't know, and again, and again each time he asked, until I was desperate and confused.

And then he shifted his questioning and began to tell me that he was my friend, that he wanted me to tell him that I wanted him to be my friend.

"I'm your friend, Tim. I can help you. Can you believe me? Will you be my friend?"

And then I broke down into tears, asking him to be my friend. He walked over to me and held me in his arms, telling me that I had made that first big step, that he would always be my friend, and that he would help me become the man I was meant to be.

That night he crawled into my sleeping bag.

~~~~

The door to the high school remains locked, and the building is empty. I've lost so much time. I've spent so much time so far away from myself.

He violated me for two and a half years. I lived a dual life. One the open unfolding of a young adult's life, and the other an unperson living in an Orwellian world of Robert's making, where freedom and understanding meant entrapment and deception.

When it was finally over, I was as adrift as I had been in my adolescence. And though I lived in the world, that teenage boy remained lost in a trauma so deep that I had no idea I was walking in shadows of my own making.

I stand up from where I was sitting in the doorway of the school and look around.

There is a breeze. The sky is blue.

My memories are wrapped in silence.

I hear my mother again: "I can't believe it! You made it! You walked all the way from Chicago just to come home!"

Kaleidoscope

When we were children, my brothers and sister and I discovered that after a rain shower the runoff from the nearby streets poured out and into the lake through a culvert that extended from the shoreline beneath a thicket of tangled bushes and small trees. What was unexpected was that the runoff from the streets above was so much cleaner than the lake, clouded as it was by a hundred years of agricultural runoff stirred up each summer by motorboats.

Over the years, as the water poured out of the culvert it carried with it the gravel spread each winter to improve traction on icy streets, as well as bits of broken glass and little pieces of twisted metal.

One hot summer day after a passing thundershower had inundated our part of town with a heavy downpour, I ran out of the house and down to the shoreline under a brightening blue sky brilliant with sunshine. I reached the thicket and made my way through to where the water was gushing out of the culvert and into the lake. I climbed naked into the cold water. I reached out and grabbed a handful of the tiny, glistening red roots that extended out of the mossy shoreline beneath the culvert.

I took a deep breath, quickly lowered my head beneath the surface, then opened my eyes, as thousands of grains of sand and broken glass roiled around me like a kaleidoscope.

Week Five

Albert Lea, MN to Minneapolis, MN

Thoreau's Cabin

The weather report is not good. But I say goodbye to my parents and leave town anyway. Minneapolis and the end of the walk lie one week to the north. A storm is expected from the south with severe winds and heavy rain, the last thrust of humid gulf air before the north wind comes down upon us with the cold and snow of winter.

The wind continues to pick up. The air is increasingly warmer and heavy with humidity. I walk faster.

The road takes a couple unexpected bends as it approaches a low ridge. Rising above the ridge stands a small knob of a hill whose sides are just steep enough to defy the plow. Looking a little pockmarked, likely excavated for gravel at one time, a vestige of prairie grass remains, hinting at the expansiveness of the Great Plains to the west sweeping across the Dakotas to the Rocky Mountains. But here in Freeborn County it is nothing more than a bit of wasteland.

Beaver Lake is just north of the Steele County line. Paul Goodnature, who agreed to let me stay at his place on Geneva Lake, is picking me up there.

On this last stretch of road, the wind rises up into gusts so strong that at times it almost trips me up. The grass growing alongside the road is bent over, showing itself greener near the ground. Like torn strips of tinfoil, silver seed heads frame fields of drying soybeans and corn, row upon row bending in unison to the wind.

The road skirts the eastern shore of Beaver Lake. I sit down on the grass at the beach and wait for Paul. It is not long before he pulls up and off we go.

Having stood in front of a classroom for forty years, Paul speaks with a voice reminiscent of the modulated tone of a musical instrument. And he laughs at just about anything. He has taught so many young people over the years that we have become variations on the same theme. We are all familiar—all our faults, all our fears, all our hopes and dreams, the details of our lives and the families we grew up in. He has heard all the songs that can be sung so many times that all he can do is laugh with the joy of understanding.

And yet despite the fact that he welcomed a constant stream of admiring students to his home for conversation, for folk music jam sessions, or just to listen to everything from Gustav Mahler to Joan Baez, lots of Joan Baez, on his carefully maintained high-fidelity stereo system, Paul cultivated a sphinxlike inscrutability. Like a priest at confession, he listened to the joys and sorrows of his students and rarely if ever pulled back the screen that separated him from all of us.

Not long after arriving at his house, we set about getting ready for a supper of burgers, potato salad, and beer on his pontoon boat out on the lake. As the sun falls closer to the horizon, the wind drops, and despite the looming presence of storm clouds to the southwest, we motor out away from the shore.

Paul shuts off the engine, and I drop anchor. As we open up our beers and Paul starts up the barbecue, I begin.

"It's funny, but I'm reminded of the backpacking trips to the Bighorn Mountains you organized when I was in high school in the seventies. Though my brother Tom and Rick Miller had made a trip out west, and I knew classmates who went along on your trips, I was never really interested. If I were to experience the wilderness, I was going to do it closer to home. So I never went much farther than the Boundary

Waters, not even to take the obligatory pilgrimage to Walden Pond."

Paul replies, "Good word choice," and we both laugh.

"And here I am," I say reflectively. "I'm walking across the Midwest, and I'm having that kind of experience."

"Yeah, and you have to realize too that in writing *Walden*, Thoreau was writing about where he could travel by foot; it was about where he lived."

Paul pauses, thinking back, then continues, "I remember the first time I ever saw you. You were sitting on the side step of your house lighting matches from a matchbook and throwing them in the grass. And the first thing I thought was, 'God, this kid must be really bored.' And then I thought it'd be interesting to see what this kid would be like in class."

We both laugh.

He says, "You know, college for me was a really liberating experience. I was raised too with a very provincial outlook on life just down the road from here in Blooming Prairie, and I was eternally grateful I went to college. I could see how other people saw things differently and that it's all right. I can look at these things, and I'm not going to burn in hell.

"And I remember the principal who hired me; his name was Red Rehwaltd. He was an incredible administrator. He took me aside before I started teaching that fall, and he said, 'These are very bright kids. You might just want to sit back and listen some of the time.' And that was good advice, I thought, in terms of respecting what people had to say. I may not always agree, but I think students knew that in my classroom what was important was that you expressed yourself."

A teacher myself for thirteen years, I know exactly what he is talking about and reply, "So you gave us the room to learn, the room to voice our opinions and explore."

He responds, "And explore, yeah."

The burgers are done now, and we are eating off of paper plates resting on our laps and sitting on lawn chairs looking out on the sky as it deepens into darker shades of blue to the north and east while to the southwest the sun has set behind an increasingly menacing storm front. But the storm still feels far enough off that we are not too worried and so keep on talking.

We continue discussing how teaching young people literature and history that suggest alternatives to what they learn in the popular media or from their parents can have a powerful effect on their developing identities and the lives they choose to live; and how learning often begins by young people rebelling against their parents.

Mulling this through, I begin, "I think I was more engaged in struggling with my parents' values and beliefs, while my older brothers got in huge arguments, screaming and yelling at them. And I think that's in part because of what we learned in junior humanities. You know, I took them on, as opposed to walking away from them."

Paul responds, "But I think your parents were stricter about their belief systems, and probably felt more threatened. Let me qualify that a little bit. I think part of it had to do with the time period, too. And I think there were probably more parents in your age group and generation who felt challenged than there were during other years when I taught the class.

"But, then again, things change. In fact—and this made me feel really good—when I got the state teacher of the year award back in 1987, the first congratulations card came from your parents. With a really nice note in it."

Thinking back, I respond, "I remember when I was in your class, they thought, 'Who is this Paul Goodnature? What kind of ideas is he filling you with? You're going where? You're going out to Paul Goodnature's house? What is that all about?' It must have been about ten or fifteen years after I graduated from high school, suddenly there was a shift. It's like, 'Oh, you know, we ran into Paul the other day.' In the past, if I had called you 'Paul,' they said, 'Paul? What's this Paul? He's not your friend; he's your teacher!' And then suddenly it was 'Paul.' It took them a while to realize that informality didn't have to suggest disrespect."

Paul again: "I run into your parents, not frequently, but you know, when I do it's really positive. That makes me feel good. I ran into your mom last year, and she said, 'It's too bad you're not teaching at the high school anymore.'

"I want to say one other thing, though. This is kind of personal. I didn't know your older brother and sister, but the other ones, the younger ones, I knew. You kids were just really intense kids."

Not sure what to make of this, I say, "Yeah?"

He continues, "You know what I'm saying? You took things seriously. There were other kids who would come into class and these ideas, they understood them, but you, man..."

I jump in, "We were hungry."

He replies, "Yeah. And you were really hungry—that's a good word for it. And every one of you has a very strong personality, a very different personality from each other, but very strong. *Hungry* is a good word. You were hungry."

As if thinking out loud, I say, "Yeah. I don't know why we were born that way."

Following this line of thinking, Paul replies, "But that's part of your personality. And I hate to say people are wired,

I just hate that expression, but there's something about it that you were just eager, eager, eager."

It is time to head back. I pull up anchor, Paul starts the engine, and we motor to shore. The thick cover of cloud in the western sky is already deepening to shades of black and gray, darker than the coming night.

Back inside his house, Paul turns on the lights as I walk around the living room looking at his photographs and artwork, much of which was given to him by former students: framed leaves, photographs of forests and mountains, paintings of rural midwestern scenes, abstract watercolors, and on the bookshelves among photographs of Paul standing with former students as well as numerous other mementos of the past are statuettes of St. Francis, the Buddha, Hindu gods and goddesses, a few kachina dolls, and an image of the Dalai Lama. Over the mantelpiece hangs a wood carving of a peace sign, a heart, and the Taoist yin and yang symbol.

Paul sits down and begins again: "I remember vividly when you called me this spring about the trip. I thought 'This kid's nuts!' I was surprised, considering your age and maturity level. You know, with your responsibility and the job you have and everything. But I thought it was refreshing that somebody would do something like what you're doing, and just take off and do it, say 'I want to do this. I'm going to do it.' I think a lot of people have dreams that never get carried out, you know.

"I hate to sound like an echo here: 'If you advance confidently in the direction of your dreams, and endeavor to live the life which you have imagined, you will meet with a success unexpected in common hours.'"

I say, "That sounds vaguely familiar. Who said that?"

Paul replies, "It comes at the end of *Walden*. It's the concluding observation about that experiment, you see.

What you've undertaken is really in that tradition. This is America. Let's get out there and see what we can learn about ourselves. And like so many of the great American writers, Vachel Lindsay, for example, they shared a passion for the country and what it had to tell them about who we are as a people.

"Lindsay had the habit of walking between performances, taking in the landscape and singing it like Walt Whitman at each performance. He pioneered performance poetry."

I reply, "I didn't know that."

He continues, "He was absorbing America, you know. And then Whitman says, 'Afoot and lighthearted, I take to the open road, healthy, free, the world before me.' And off you go. So, I mean, you're doing it in your particular area or region, your experience, which is what they had done."

"And that's why it's so rich with the American experience. So, I mean, you're part of that culture; you're just extending it and bringing it into the modern age, which most people wouldn't do today. In fact, some would say, 'No car?' And Henry walked into Boston instead of taking the train because he figured out that in the time he'd need to work to buy the ticket, he could walk there and absorb it all."

I reply, "I'd like to think that this walk had something to do with the American authors I read in your class. And though I didn't think about it ahead of time, I shouldn't be surprised that this experience has been so silent and so introspective. It's as if the walk has led me back to where my life blends with the land upon which I've lived. So maybe I'll have something to say as well."

Paul replies, "Well, see, now you've come full circle. You know it's too much to keep to yourself; you have to write a book. Tim, I've got to say, though I'm surprised you're here, I'm not that surprised. You're a Herwig, after all."

We both laugh.

I say good night and walk over to the cabin. Paul does not have a spare bedroom, but he does have a guesthouse: a replica of the cabin Henry David Thoreau built on the shores of Walden Pond. He and a group of former students built it.

The cabin has no electricity so Paul sends me over with a flashlight. Inside I see through its narrow beam that the interior walls are covered with varnished wooden paneling. There is a woodstove in one corner and a set of four wooden chairs in a circle on a rag rug in the middle of the room. Above is a sleeping loft accessible only by a narrow ladder. A small bookcase stands at the back of the room with what looks like books on Walden and the life of Thoreau and other American authors. On the wall hangs my most favorite of Paul's works of art: a drawing of a cabin among a grove of pines done entirely using the word *Walden*. A student before my time had done it and presented it to Paul as a gift. I have always greatly admired it and noticed that it was not hanging in his house. It is a relief to see it here.

Before I climb into my sleeping bag, I turn on the flashlight, and find a copy of *Walden*. Paging through what seems the same edition I read in high school, I find a passage that has always stayed with me. "A lake is the landscape's most beautiful and expressive feature. It is earth's eye; looking into which the beholder measures the depth of his own nature."

I think about my conversation with Paul. How much like daylight he seems. In Paul's eyes there has been no break in the continuity of my life. I have a voice. I have the voice I have always had.

The Wind and the Rain

The next morning, Paul drops me off back at Beaver Lake, and we say our goodbyes. The road carries me due north for several miles under an overcast sky and through heavy sheets of mist-like rain. Then the road shifts off the grid through a dismal stretch of wasteland. As I walk down gravel roads in mud-caked shoes, the rain falls heavier and heavier.

In just one night, the fields have shifted closer to autumn and harvest time. Many of the soybean fields have begun to turn gold, while the grass alongside the road is increasingly brown and gray.

It begins to thunder, and lightning strikes the fields in the distance. I make my way to a motel along Interstate 35 north of Owatonna. Five more miles along a gravel road turned to mud by the unrelenting downpour. Suddenly the road crosses a line out from between farm fields and onto a paved, curbed street with mowed grass growing on either side. It is as if I have emerged out of the wilderness and into the suburbs.

~~~~

The motel's automatic doors open, then close behind me. Once inside, overwhelmed by a wave of intense air conditioning, I am immediately chilled to a state of near hypothermia. Despite manufacturer's claims that the rain gear breathes, I am drenched with sweat beneath and completely wet on the outside. At the front desk, I am greeted by a young woman who is vacantly happy to help me.

She gathers the requisite information at a near glacial pace.

I interrupt and try to hurry her along. "I've just walked twenty miles. I'm soaked and freezing in this crazy air conditioning. Please, just give me the key so I can get to my room?"

She asks, "May I please have the license number of your car?"

I think, *I'm standing in front of her dressed in rain gear with a large pack on my back and a wide-brimmed hat on my head dripping water on the counter, and she asks me for the license number of my car.*

I tell her, "I walked here. I don't have a car."

Without missing a beat: "Do you need one key card or two?"

She hands me the one I request and directs me to the elevators. "We offer a complimentary breakfast between 6:00 AM and 10:00 AM each morning. You're welcome to enjoy it. I hope you enjoy your stay."

I take a thirty-minute hot shower.

Before I crawl into bed, I open the curtains then turn off the lights. It is foggy outside. The lights in the parking lot glow eerily through the grey mists. I lie in bed, listen to the air conditioner, and look out the window.

Some parts of my experience with Robert are harder to bring to mind than others. When it began, my sister and all my brothers except for Paul had moved away. We were the only two left.

One night, I sat alone at the kitchen table with my parents. They began questioning me about Robert, questions that I either didn't answer or answered with lies.

They don't understand what Robert and I have together. They can't know what it means to be an educated person. All dad is interested in is sports and mom her Readers Digest Condensed Books.

My dad asks angrily, "What is it you're doing with that teacher at all hours of the night? Why would a grown man want to spend all his time with a high school student?"

I answer, "We sit in the basement and talk about books and listen to music. He's teaching me about important ideas, about philosophy and history."

My mother jumps in, "And where is his wife this whole time? What woman would let her husband spend so much time with one of his students alone in the basement?"

I answer feeling nervous and angry. I know they cannot understand. I am afraid to tell them the truth. "She's upstairs watching TV."

I do not tell them that she is upstairs drinking. I do not tell them that Robert is drinking too. I do not tell them that he is naked beneath a terry cloth robe. I do not tell them that he places a jar of Vaseline on the table next to his drink. I do not tell them what happens next, over and again, every night I'm over to his house. I do not tell them how utterly lost I am.

Yelling at them, "I'm not going to stop going over there, and you can't stop me."

That was it. They got up from the table and left the room. They never again asked me about Robert and what I was doing over there. I told them about ten years later. We were sitting once again at the kitchen table. I asked them did they know Robert sexually abused me. Faced with a truth they didn't want to know, they responded with shame and guilt. My mother went on and on about what a terrible mother she was. My dad said, "It must have been hard for you to live with this all these years."

The night after my parents questioned me, I told everything to Robert. He got angry. Whether out of fear of discovery or a need to exercise power, he told me that he was coming over the next night to tell my parents that their unspoken suspicions were unfounded. They were cowards. They were ignorant cowards.

For Robert, the sex, or so he claimed, was all about preparing me for relationships with women. He was teaching me not only about the ideas that shaped Western culture, but how to become a sensualist. He was liberating my mind and body.

I told my parents the next day that Robert was coming over that night. They could hardly comprehend what I told them. They knew something was very wrong. But they were afraid to face it. They wanted someone to convince them they were wrong. They were paralyzed by the fear of what was happening to me, but chose to do nothing about it.

Robert arrived that evening. We all sat in the living room: my parents on either end of the couch and Robert and I in chairs on either side the room facing them. Robert began talking.

He told them they were wrong to question his intentions. He told them nothing they suspected was going on. He was teaching me. I was very bright and sensitive, and he was helping me grow into my potential. He told them I came over of my own volition. He wasn't forcing me to do anything I didn't want.

I watched in silence as he talked. He sat there lying to my parents, and I said nothing. When he was finished, my parents were in shock. Like two birds hypnotized by a cat, they were devoured by a lie posing as the truth.

When he got up to leave, my dad said out loud to himself, "Five sons and not one of them an athlete."

I watch the weather report. The forecast is for continued heavy rain, wind gusts in excess of forty miles an hour, and more thunderstorm activity. I fall asleep apprehensive about what lies ahead.

~~~~

The southwest wind is angry.
Walking west, it pushes me into oncoming traffic.
Walking north, almost off my feet.
Into the west once more, the wind
Blows me across the road
Into the ditch.
Cars race by.
Into the wind.

~~~~

An egg-shaped sward of green grass
At the center of a soybean field,
Motionless
Within windswept
Brushstrokes of yellow, orange, and pink
Framed by drying grass
Fading from silver to lilac.

~~~~

Cannon Lake is one among a chain of lakes that forms the upper reaches of the Cannon River watershed. The river flows northeast from the Faribault area to just north of Red Wing, where it enters the Mississippi. A state hiking trail runs for a couple miles through a tree-covered corridor along the south shore of the lake.

The wind continues to blow, and for a brief time the cloud cover opens up, revealing a bright blue sky behind rows of fast-moving clouds. The trees blow violently, strewing twigs and leaves across the path and breaking up the light so that the green-walled enclosure feels on the verge of being torn apart.

The World Goes Round

for C.A.R.

I arrive at Roberds Lake Resort at the end of the day after walking more than twenty miles. The resort is empty of people. It is off-season. All the kids have gone back to school.

Everything is painted red. Inside the lodge is a wide-open, multipurpose room with concrete floors, tables and chairs for eating, games for the kids, and at the center a counter from which food and drink are served from an open grill and kitchen.

The owners are not particularly friendly. They had not expected any paying guests. I ask for something to eat, but the kitchen is closed. I ask again, and they reluctantly agree to cook me up some burgers and fries, for which I am very grateful.

I am staying in cabin number six, one bedroom for sixty-five dollars a night. They direct me to the cabin, lock up, and retire to their own home. A row of cabins stretches out on a low ridge overlooking the main lodge and the lake beyond.

The cabin is small and damp. The knotty pine paneling is stained in a washed-out beige.

I sit quietly on the bed. All the vacationers are gone. No more lounging at the lake. No more running around after dark with summer friends, stealing food from the lodge or kisses from the girls. No more getting up at dawn to motor out on the lake, cast a line, and sit watching the sunrise burn off the mist, opening up the sky to that infinite blue in which we all live.

Everyone is back at work or school but me. I sit alone in this cabin with nothing to keep me company but the stillness of my own quieted thoughts; and now they drift off, and I am here alone with the stillness: breathing in, breathing out, breathing in, breathing out.

When I was a boy, I was afraid of being left alone in the school building on the last day before summer vacation. As soon as the bell rang, I shot out of the classroom, down the stairs, and out the door before any of my classmates. Once across the street, I looked back with my heart racing and sweat trickling down my skin beneath my shirt.

But here I am now all these years later, sitting alone in that classroom, alone in that empty school, listening to the creaking of an old building that long ago had settled in and learned the slow, almost imperceptible movements of the earth, until those sounds fall away and all that is left is the beating of my heart and the sound of my breathing.

I get up and walk outside. The sun has begun its descent toward the western horizon. It is much colder than earlier in the day, so I quickly walk back and put on every stitch of clothing I have. I zip on my pant legs, put on my fleece vest, my rain jacket over that. And then I walk from the cabin down the slope, across the road, then out from beneath the trees and onto a long dock that extends out over the water. The wind has shifted out of the south and is now blowing just as strongly from the west-northwest.

The tree-lined western shore is already backlit to black, the sky above silver and blue beyond wind-torn clouds of black, gray, and white. I stand there watching the shifting clouds, the silver light, and the slowly deepening blue sky that lies above. The particularities of nature have given way to bold shapes and forms breaking away from, then blending into each other, creating yet more shapes that, as time passes, deepen, then disappear into the night.

I look down and see that I am bathed in the most beautiful golden light. Everything around me, the docks extended out over the choppy waters of the lake, the trees behind them blown about by the wind, the bright facades of the houses that lie beneath a canopy of golden-edged leaves of green—everything along the eastern shoreline of the lake is illuminated in the warmest possible light, in increasingly sharper contrast to the cloud-shattered western sky, deepening into shades of purple, pink, and gray.

I am a still point in a moving landscape changing with the season.

Here I stand at the top of the watershed, at the confluence of past and present, personal and otherness, where golden light and violent storm meet, where summer gives way to autumn, where the entire landscape is put in motion by the same wind that fills our lungs.

Here I stand, watching the sky, the clouds, the silver light before me, the golden light behind.

Here I stand, watching the waves roll toward me and the trees swaying in the wind along the shoreline.

Here I stand, listening to the wind in the waves before me and the wind in the trees behind.

Here I stand, and from deep within my body upwells a reservoir of quiet.

For years I looked for something that I could not find. I have been looking for that part of myself suspended by the trauma I suffered as a teenager. My life and my voice were hushed, nothing happened. I could put myself there and look out at the world and watch it move by. I had stepped out of time or had somehow slowed it down so that everything else around me moved just fast enough that the difference reinforced my separateness.

And then I forgot and was forgotten by the world. I ruminated on my absence and thought it introspection. I spoke a language that was not mine, but his.

Robert reached so deep inside me and yanked out something so fundamental that I lost myself in the emptiness left behind. I was lost in a geology of absence deep inside my body. And there I spent years in the dark looking for that part of myself that was taken from me—the ever-flowing river without beginning or end always emerging but never to emerge, youth, change, love, the living of life.

But in that moment of stillness, I find that lost teenager. I hold him in my arms, listening to the silence for the longest time before we walk together back out into the light of this day. And here I am awash in the golden light of the setting sun, borne on a wind from the northwest carrying with it a darkness that no longer lives inside me.

"I Heard There Was a Party…"

On the last day, I walk out of the country, through the suburbs, and into the city of Minneapolis. My goal: a backyard party at a friend's house.

Late that afternoon, I turn up the front walk, step into the backyard, and announce to all those gathered, "I heard there was a party, so I thought I'd walk over!"

We all cheer, and I cry as I hug and kiss everyone all around. *I made it.*

I began by thinking I was walking home. But now I understand that the home I walked to is the life I lost so long ago. I can now hear in my own words the future calling out to me. Calling out to me to return to Chicago.

I have another beer and declare my love for everyone present, joyous in the peace I have found in a landscape of love in which I am now free to live.

Kathy

When I returned to Chicago not a lot changed. I worked the same job, lived in the same apartment, and lived my life much as I had done before walking to Minnesota. Yet if I thought about the walk, the quiet, the wind and sky, the flowing water returned to me and I smiled. I lived my ordinary life and smiled.

Less than a year later, I met Kathy online. We were ones and zeros and then one day materialized on the front steps of her apartment building.

Time passed, and I asked her to go out with me. She said yes. A little after that, I asked her if she would like to be girlfriend and boyfriend. She said yes again. And even though it was obvious to everyone else, most especially Kathy, that I was falling in love with her, I couldn't quite figure it out. And then one day, I did.

~~~~

I think to myself, I'm falling in love with Kathy,
But can't find the words to describe how it feels.
And then I do.
This time love feels like water.
Our love is cool water flowing
From shade into sunlight.

Acknowledgements

Thank you to the many people who helped me with both the walk and the book. I may have walked and wrote the book alone, but everything else was a conversation.

- Amy Garcengel and Andy Cengel. Amy and Andy encouraged me to undertake the walk at a moment when I was ready to listen.
- Deirdre Schmidt. Calling up her extensive experience running marathons, Deidre helped me develop and training program that prepared me well for the walk.
- Tim Murakami. We spent many lunches together talking about our lives and the machinations of work. During one lunch, he suggested I drive the route I had chosen ahead of time. It saved me a lot of wrong turns along my way.
- Rachel Mann. Rachel rode with me when I drove the first half of the route taking note of places to stay, eat, and the location of post offices to which I would mail supplies. Her love, empathy, and ability to listen helped me make sense of what I was about to do.
- Christine Petersen. Chris insisted that I call her every morning of each day to let her know that I was alive and had not been run over and left for dead in a ditch somewhere. Chris's sense of humor, open heart, and capacity to listen to every detail of my broken heart was more than anyone should expect of another.

- Tim Bailey. At one point Tim was the president of the bank where I worked. We had weekly meetings during which we were supposed to talk about community development. Inevitably we talked about theology, God, faith, free market capitalism and whether government regulation should have any part in it, and the open road. Tim is a Harley Davidson enthusiast with a keen appreciation of distance. When I told him I planned to take off six weeks from work to walk to Minnesota, he replied "Go for it."

- Paul Jarosz. Paul and his wife put me up for a night in suburban Chicago. Paul picked me up outside the Maywood Racetrack and brought me back the next day.

- Mark and Becca Gault. Not only did they let me park my car in their driveway when I was out on the road, but they also met me in Byron, IL to spend a little time together. An incident involving ice cream on an island in the middle of the Mississippi will live forever in our memories.

- Mike and Lisa Johnstone. Mike and Lisa met me in Mineral Point, WI. They brought duct tape to tape up my shoes. It's impossible not to have fun with them. We said our goodbyes on the road. I walked on and they turned their car around and drove off in the opposite direction.

- Aaron Rubenstein and Patrick Scully. Two dear friends who walked with me for two days in southern Minnesota. Aaron Rubenstein also hosted the backyard party at the end of the walk. Thank you to all the friends and family who attended.

- Mark McKelvey and Loren Niemi. Mark and Loren also walked with me for part of a day: Mark in Chicago and Loren in the southern suburbs of Minneapolis.

- Rick Herwig and Roxanne Snyder. My brother and sister-in-law put me up for a night in Burnsville, MN. The next morning Rick drove me across the Minnesota River as there was no safe way of doing so on foot.
- Pamela Bingham: Perhaps most importantly, Pam through her integrative, therapeutic massage after the walk, helped me rid my body of the vestiges of my trauma. Without her, the love I share with Kathy and Forrest's very existence would never have been possible.
- At a low point, I volunteered to Andre Feriante that I had decided to create a website, post the most recent version of the book (clearly not ready for publication), and be done with it. Andre asked me what was most important. I told him the text. He told me to do nothing more until I was satisfied that the book was as excellent as I could make it. I followed his advice, and here I am. Thanks Andre.
- Thank you to all the people I met on the road whose conversations unexpectedly and almost without exception guided me on my way.

I am grateful to the many friends and family members who read the manuscript at varying points in its development and provided me with invaluable criticism and counsel. They include Ammar Askari, Jane Barnes, Pam Bingham, Sara Belleau, Djola Branner, Bart Buch, Craig Cox, Kay Ann Criswell, Rajive Das, Moe Flaherty, Paul Ginger, Paul Goodnature, Marty Grochala, Kathy Herwig, Paul Herwig, Johanna Hynes, Jennifer Ilse, Delia Jobst, Jennifer Jobst, Joe Jobst, Sue Jobst, Deirdre McCloskey, Timothy Mennel, Keith Morton, Loren Niemi, Sharon Parker, Shannon Pennefeather, Catherine Pines, Fred Reuland, Stephanie Roland, Letty Shapiro, Bonnie Mortimore Smith, Jolyn Thompson, Charles Thornbury, Aaron Rubenstein, Tricia Welsch, Kevin

Whiteley, Tracy Whiteley, Betsy Wulff, and for those I may have forgotten please accept my apologies and gratitude.

I would especially like to thank Craig Cox and Loren Niemi who have been with me since the beginning. Thanks for taking endless cries for help, advice, and editorial support. We did it guys! I also want to thank my former colleague, Paul Ginger. He had the misfortune of having an office across the corridor from mine for nearly 15 years. He got it all and then some! Thanks for being a good sport. I would also like to give special thanks to my former English Professor Charles Thornbury. I'm honored to have benefited from his sophisticated and subtle reading of the manuscript.

Thank you to Greg Britton who is now Editorial Director, Johns Hopkins University Press Books. Greg read a compilation of letters I wrote from the road that appeared in the Minneapolis Observer, called me up, and said "I read your letters and was left with a lot of questions. And then I thought, if I got answers to these questions there could be a book. Have you ever thought about writing a book?"

Thank you to Richard Fox who provided invaluable guidance on book design, and to artist Chuck Myers for his wonderful painting on the outside cover of the book.

I never wrote down my performance pieces because I wanted to keep them fresh in my mind. After a performance early in the 1990s, my friend Molly Wieland asked, "Tim, have you ever thought about writing down your performances? I think they would make great stories." It had never occurred to me to do so. That's when it all began. Thanks Molly!

Thank you also to Andrew Carey, publisher of Triarchy Press. If he hadn't acceded to my demand to sit down in his easy chair and read the book, no matter how busy he was, none of this would have happened!

And finally, of course, thank you to my wife Kathy and our son Forrest for your love, patience, companionship, and constant reminder that even for a writer, family always comes first.

About the Author

Though *The Long Way Home* is my first published book, I have been a writer, performer, teacher, and student of literature and the humanities for all my adult life. Most important to me was the period in which I was a performance artist. As a performing artist, I was interested in how a poet or writer transforms an image into metaphor. I imagined a physical space or moment of time between the formation of a metaphor and when a writer or poet writes it on a piece of paper or taps it out on a keyboard. I wanted to emote for an audience the first words of discovery.

It is in this spirit that I wrote *The Long Way Home*. I have tried to imagine the present moment using the power of discovery to invite the reader into the same experience. Wherever possible, I've used context to inform each image with meaning rather than explaining its importance. I hope this approach will help readers imagine and understand my experience and also to imagine themselves undergoing a similar experience of self-discovery.

I also worked for many years in the social/economic justice field of community development. In that time, I worked both for a bank and a federal regulatory agency. Community development largely came about because of the passage of the Community Reinvestment Act in 1977. It is the last major piece of federal civil rights legislation. Through it, the federal government monitors the extent to which banks provide access to financial services for low- and moderate-income people and low- and moderate-income communities. Because of the historic correlation between race and poverty in America, this has meant working primarily in communities of color. In my final years, I worked on community development in economically distressed communities in the rural Midwest.

I live in the City of Chicago with my wife and our son.

Also available from Triarchy Press

A Sardine Street Box of Tricks ~ Crab Man & Signpost
Counter-Tourism: A Pocketbook & Handbook ~ Phil Smith
Covert: A Handbook ~ Melanie Kloetzel & Phil Smith
Desire Paths ~ Roy Bayfield
Enchanted Things ~ Phil Smith
Guidebook for an Armchair Pilgrimage ~ John Schott et al.
Making Routes ~ Laura Bissell & David Overend
Mythogeography ~ Phil Smith
On Walking... and Stalking Sebald ~ Phil Smith
Rethinking Mythogeography ~ John Schott & Phil Smith
Terminalian Drift ~ Jerry Gordon
The Architect-Walker ~ Wrights & Sites
The Footbook of Zombie Walking ~ Phil Smith
The MK Myth ~ Phil Smith & K
The Pattern: a fictioning ~ Helen Billinghurst & Phil Smith
walk write (repeat) ~ Sonia Overall
Walking Art Practice ~ Ernesto Pujol
Walking Bodies ~ Helen Billinghurst, Claire Hind, Phil Smith
Walking for Creative Recovery ~ Christina Reading & Jess Moriarty
Walking's New Movement ~ Phil Smith
Walking Stumbling Limping Falling ~ Alyson Hallett & Phil Smith
Ways to Wander ~ Claire Hind & Clare Qualmann
Ways to Wander the Gallery ~ Claire Hind & Clare

www.triarchypress.net/walking

Reflections

The Long Way Home gives new meaning to Emerson's words: "It's not the destination, it's the journey." As Herwig opens to the land during his quest for that elusive state of being known as home, he opens to memories of childhood, family, and to the histories of all the idiosyncratic people he encounters along the way. His photographic journey transcends time and place in the best possible way, and ultimately leads him right back where he belongs.

– Djola Branner
Professor of Theater, George Mason University. His first book of collected plays, sash & trim and other plays, *was a finalist for the Lambda Literary Award in 2014*

Seeking to exorcise demons both recent and enduring, Tim Herwig set out to walk from his adopted home of Chicago into the arms of friends and family 500 miles north. Along the way, he rediscovers a sense of self with the help of dozens of ordinary Midwesterners who share their own trials and triumphs. Part aching memoir, part meticulous travelogue, *The Long Way Home* is both a masterful portrait of small-town America and an inspiring tale of hard-earned redemption.

– Craig Cox, author of Storefront Revolution: Food Co-ops and the Counterculture

Intensely personal, Herwig's *The Long Way Home* describes the long and literal walking journey he takes as an adult to his home in Minnesota. While doing so, he recalls in vivid details the significant and life changing events of his past in this coming-of-age story. Young readers will find comfort and hope in the stories of challenge and triumph while more mature ones will find themselves reflecting on their own journeys as they, like Herwig, are inspired to discover their way home to the people they are.

– Paul Goodnature, teacher, Humanities, Albert Lea Senior High School. 1987 Minnesota Teacher of the Year

Timothy Herwig illuminates the literature of walking with profound observation and self-contemplation. His curiosity about, and love of, people, land and history shines through every word. What makes this book particularly special is that as Tim journeys, he realizes that, at least in part, it is helping him heal from the trauma of teenage sexual abuse and a painful, fractured marriage. The landscape, weather and individuals he meets entertain, cajole, nurture, threaten, and push him to go deeper into memories and dreams. He wrestles with his demons, even while Mother Nature guides and holds him in a safe space until he comes at the end of his journey to a place of peace. Tim's humility, honesty, transparency, and authenticity is deeply engaging and refreshing. You walk with him and see yourself. As a therapist/healer who helps people heal from trauma and find a spiritual light within nature to guide their life, I highly recommend this book. It shines like a brilliant gem into the soul.

– Rachel Mann PhD, Sacred Activist, Social Scientist, Healer and Spiritual Teacher, rachelmannphd.com

The Long Way Home is an authentically and beautifully rendered memoir of the internal trauma that results when adult mentors sexually violate the vulnerable youth who trust them. More importantly, it is the story of what healing is like—a literal and metaphoric journey that ends with wholeness, but a wholeness imbued with a wisdom that comes from stepping into what is most feared. It is not a book about winning over or vanquishing the past—it is a book about accepting that the past can't be undone, while showing that it can be disarmed and embraced, gingerly, in our own journeys. *The Long Way Home* is about the potential that comes when we trust our bodies to heal our minds and hearts and is an example of the gifts that come from reflecting deeply and honestly on our experiences of the world around us. Without sentimentality or cliché, *The Long Way Home* invites us to imagine our own journeys to being at peace with ourselves and with the world as it is.

> *– Keith Morton, Professor of Public and Community Services at Providence College. Author of* Getting Out: Youth Gangs, Violence, and Positive Change

Tim Herwig's journey from Chicago to Minneapolis is more than a memoir of a walk across several of the United States, it is also a traversing of states of mind, the poetic sense of time, place and light, and a lyric evocation of geography and history (both cultural and personal). Reading this is to know both the man and the Midwest he clearly loves.

> *Loren Niemi, Storyteller / Author of* What Haunts Us, *winner of the 2020 Midwest Book award for 'Sci-Fi / Fantasy / Horror / Paranormal Fiction'*

The Long Way Home is a remarkable treasure of exquisitely crafted prose that reads like poetry. As he walks from Illinois to Minnesota, Tim Herwig describes his journey in vivid detail with glorious and highly informative descriptions of geography, history, landscapes, trees and plants, architecture, and rural life. This is also the record of a journey of coming home to the self as the author walks through childhood ghosts, an exploration of his past, and ultimately finds a new sense of place and home within.

> *– Catherine Pines, Ph.D., DePaul University Family and Community Services, Coordinator of Training (emeritus)*